STANDING

The Story of Bryan

STANDING FOR GOD
The Story of Elijah

Roger Ellsworth

THE BANNER OF TRUTH TRUST

THE BANNER OF TRUTH TRUST
3 Murrayfield Road, Edinburgh EH12 6EL
P.O. Box 621, Carlisle, Pennsylvania 17013, USA

*

© Roger Ellsworth 1994
First Published 1994
ISBN 0 85151 665 3

*

Typeset in 11/13pt Monotype Bembo
Printed and bound in Great Britain by
BPC Paperbacks Ltd
A member of
The British Printing Company Ltd

TO TIM AND MARTY
Sons after the flesh
Brothers after the Spirit

CONTENTS

INTRODUCTION

The prophet Elijah might be called 'the man without a resume.' He bursts onto the stage of human history with only these words of introduction: 'And Elijah the Tishbite, of the inhabitants of Gilead, said to Ahab: "As the Lord God of Israel lives, before whom I stand, there shall not be dew nor rain these years, except at my word"' (*1 Kings* 17:1).

While his appearance is indeed very abrupt it should not take us by surprise. The nation of Israel, with King Ahab at its helm, had lurched into an exceedingly dark and treacherous hour, an hour that is amply described for us in the verses immediately preceding the appearance of Elijah (16:29-34). This hour was dark and treacherous because it coupled a deep disdain for the Word of God with the introduction of the worship of Baal into the nation's life.

Many in Israel did not see the issue clearly. They thought it possible to retain the worship of God and at the same time make room for the worship of Baal. The latter could be recognized as the god who controlled weather and growth, and the rest of life could be assigned to the God of their fathers.

Elijah refused to be taken in by such fanciful notions. He knew the God of Israel was sovereign over every aspect of life and would allow no rivals. In his sudden appearance before Ahab he threw the gauntlet down by saying God would demonstrate from the realm that Ahab and the nation had assigned to Baal that He alone was God and no synthesis was possible.

All of this may seem to be of value only to those who nurture some quaint interest in the history of ancient kings and kingdoms. The truth is, however, that the struggle between Elijah and Ahab is being played out again in our own day and age. Many seem to be in love with the idea of synthesizing the Word of God with the secular mindset of our age. The life of Elijah speaks to us at this point by reminding us of God's sovereignty over all. It also speaks to those who have rejected the idea of synthesis by seeking to remain true to the Word of God. The life of Elijah speaks to all God's faithful people to not grow discouraged in the struggle because God's cause is going to ultimately prevail.

This book is, therefore, primarily addressed to Christians, but it is my hope that the sad spectacle of the godless Ahab and his terrible end, coupled with the glorious picture of Elijah walking in close fellowship with the God of heaven, will cause any reader who does not know Christ to flee to him in repentance and faith.

The chapters of this book were originally preached to my beloved congregation, the Immanuel Baptist Church of Benton, Illinois. I deeply appreciate the warm love these people constantly show for the Word of God and for their pastor who seeks to preach it.

I am especially indebted to my wife, Sylvia, and to my secretary, Sheila Ketteman, for their help in making this book possible. My prayer is that the God of Elijah will be honoured through these pages.

1

Standing for God in Apostate Times

In the thirty-eighth year of Asa king of Judah, Ahab the son of Omri became king over Israel; and Ahab the son of Omri reigned over Israel in Samaria twenty-two years. Now Ahab the son of Omri did evil in the sight of the LORD, more than any all who were before him. And it came to pass, as though it had been a trivial thing for him to walk in the sins of Jeroboam the son of Nebat, that he took as his wife Jezebel the daughter of Ethbaal, king of the Sidonians; and he went and served Baal and worshiped him. Then he set up an altar for Baal in the temple of Baal, which he had built in Samaria. And Ahab made a wooden image. Ahab did more to provoke the LORD God of Israel to anger than all the kings of Israel who were before him.

1 Kings 16:29-33

The word 'apostasy' comes from the Greek word 'apostasia', which consists of the prefix *apo* meaning 'from' and the root word *histasthai* which means 'stand'. Apostasy literally means, then, 'moving away from one's stand' or 'to stand away from'. The word has been used to describe a soldier deserting his post.

Within the context of our analysis, apostasy refers to the renunciation or abandonment of both the teachings and the practice of Christianity by those who previously professed faith in and allegiance to Jesus Christ. In 2 Thessalonians 2:3 Paul says there will be a time of unprecedented apostasy as we approach the end of time. From what we see and hear around us, it is easy to believe we are already in the early stages of that apostasy. Many who once professed faith in the Lord Jesus Christ have turned away to embrace false doctrines and to practise ungodly living.

In his book, *What Americans Believe*, George Barna documents the scope of this apostasy. He finds, for instance, that 77 percent of evangelical Christians believe people are basically good; and only 56 percent of those who claim to have made a personal commitment to Christ are dependent upon that commitment for their salvation.[1] Both of these views are completely contradictory to orthodox Christianity.

Some Christians try to respond to the gale-force wind of apostasy by simply ignoring it and pretending all is well; some respond by trying to create a synthesis between the doctrines of the Bible and the popular beliefs of the day; while others try to keep their religious faith in a separate compartment, completely away from daily life, so that they feel no tension. But many Christians are keenly aware of the epidemic proportions

1   Barna, George, *What Americans Believe, An Annual Survey of Values and Religious Views in the United States*, Regal Books, 1991, pp. 88–91, 195–196.

of apostasy and are seeking strength to cope with it. They find it is not easy to live in an age of apostasy, and even though they have been able to maintain their faith they find themselves discouraged, weary, hesitant, confused, timid and uncertain. They feel just like the meagre band of disciples who were left standing around Jesus after the vast multitude had departed (*John* 6:60-71). How could so many be wrong? How could so few be right?

The account of Elijah will serve as a tonic for all of those who are beleaguered and befuddled by the curse of apostasy because the great message of Elijah's ministry is simply this: God's cause, no matter how bleak the outlook, will never fail, and those who remain faithful to him will finally be vindicated. We all tend to think our own age is more challenging than any other, but no one has ever lived in bleaker times than Elijah.

The nation of Israel, led by King Ahab, was firmly in the clutches of idolatry which, although unprecedented in extent, had been a recurrent characteristic of God's people since the break-up of the united kingdom forged under David and ruled over by Solomon. Because of the foolishness of Solomon's son, Rehoboam, the ten northern tribes had rebelled against him and established Israel. Two tribes remained true to Rehoboam and became known as the kingdom of Judah (*1 Kings* 12:1-19).

Shortly after Jeroboam successfully led this revolt against Rehoboam, he became concerned about his subjects going back to Jerusalem to worship in Solomon's temple. He thought his kingdom could not last long if the people continued to worship in Judah, so he set up golden calves at two locations and established his own priesthood (*1 Kings* 12:27-33). Jeroboam was followed by five kings who refused to repudiate the idolatry he had introduced. Then Ahab ascended

3

the throne, and under his leadership Israel entered into a form of idolatry which made the lapses of Jeroboam and his five successors appear trifling in comparison. The Bible tells us 'he went and served Baal and worshiped him' (*1 Kings* 16:31), and he 'made a wooden image' (verse 33).

Baal was the chief god of the Canaanite nations. He was considered to be the god of nature who caused the land to be fertile. Therefore he was the god of weather and growth. According to the popular beliefs of that day, Baal could actually be seen in thunderstorms. The wooden image Ahab made was of a Canaanite goddess who was believed to control vegetation and life. By relating sexually to this goddess, Baal produced fertility in the land. It is not surprising, then, that sex played a large part in the worship of Baal. Both male and female prostitutes were available at the temple of Baal so each worshipper could act out the marriage of Baal to the land. This re-enactment, along with a gift to Baal, assured the worshipper fertile land and a good crop.

The enormity of these developments must not be lost on us. The people of Israel were not mere Canaanites. They were the people the Lord had set apart for himself and with whom he had established a covenant. And the king of Israel was no ordinary monarch. He was a theocratic king; that is, he was charged with ruling the people on behalf of God himself and as God's representative.

But why should Ahab's idolatry be considered worse than that of his predecessors? Because he introduced an idolatry of a different and much more dangerous character. The golden calves built by Jeroboam and allowed by his successors were wrong, but they were still part of the worship of the true God. They were intended as aids to the worship of God not as replacements for it. But Ahab's idolatry brought in a completely new god altogether.

This is not to say that Ahab intended to replace completely the worship of God. The names of Ahab's children (Ahaziah, Jehoram and Athaliah) all contained an element of the Hebrew name for God, Jahweh. In all probability, Ahab thought both Baal and God could be worshipped at the same time without conflict. How often God's people make the very same mistake! How often we think we can accommodate the false without harming the true: the theory of evolution was developed and some began to try to synthesize it with the biblical account of creation; new theories of sexuality came along and attempts were made to synthesize them with the teachings of the Bible on sexual morality; a new emphasis on self-esteem became fashionable and immediately some people began to synthesize it with the Bible's teachings about man's sinful nature.

All these attempts at synthesis give the impression that we are content for God to have a place in our lives, so long as he is out of view and does not interfere with how we actually live. The trouble with this approach is that it does not come to grips with his sovereign rule over all. He is the one who gives us our place, and he demands that we give him our lives, not simply a place in our lives.

How are we to explain Ahab's bringing the worship of Baal into Israel and trying to create a new religious synthesis? The answer to this question is found in these sombre words: 'he took as wife Jezebel the daughter of Ethbaal, king of the Sidonians' (verse 31).

Jezebel! Here was the source of much of Ahab's evil. The name of her father was 'Ethbaal' which meant 'with him is Baal', and her name meant 'Baal is the prince'. Such names leave no doubt about where the sympathies of Jezebel and her father lay. Ahab may have been interested in a synthesis between Baal and God, but Jezebel was interested in nothing

5

less than Baal's being worshipped without rival. She was uncompromising in her commitment to Baal.

One of the great ironies of our day is that Christians claim to be recipients of God's revealed truth, and yet so often are eager to accommodate popular opinion and reluctant to call people to God. They do not want to be accused of being dogmatic or of imposing their faith on others. But while they are being so modest about the Bible's message, other groups are militant about their own beliefs. They show no reluctance in claiming the absolute truth of their views. A further irony is that while Christians are so concerned to incorporate into their beliefs the viewpoints of such groups, Christianity's opponents have absolutely no interest in returning the favour. While Christians scurry around trying to make room in their doctrines for the latest fad, the secularists of our day, like Jezebel, have a totalitarian commitment that will not rest until all rivals have been vanquished.

But if Ahab was a syncretist and Jezebel was an absolutist, why did he ever marry her? There is no great mystery here. It was both the common practice of his day and politically expedient! By marrying into each other's families, kings formed political alliances that could prove very valuable in terms of trade and military strength! On the face of things, these reasons appear compelling enough. What could possibly be wrong with a king strengthening himself both economically and militarily?

Here again we must not lose sight of the fact that Israel was in a different situation and under a different set of rules. The fact that a particular course of action was commonplace among other nations and appeared to bring political advantages was irrelevant for a nation that was to be ruled by the Word of God. Only one thing matters among such a people, and that is what God says. Israel was to learn through bitter experience that there were no advantages gained in ignoring God's Word.

The same is true today. God's people will never be able to function as they ought and to accomplish what they should until they reach the point where they do not mind being different. Christians must constantly guard against the temptation to minimize the difference between themselves and the world. The glory of Christianity is in that difference!

Elijah has not yet appeared on the stage, but we are already confronted with powerful lessons. One is that we must always be on guard against the temptation to water down our faith so that it will be acceptable to a godless age. Synthesis may appear to be an attractive option, but it is a dead end street. Jesus himself warned us that, 'No one can serve two masters' (*Matt.* 6:24).

Another lesson to be gained from Ahab's folly is that we must always vigilantly avoid relationships with evil people. There is no doubt that Jezebel had a profound influence on Ahab and took him farther down the road of idolatry than he would have gone without her.

Closely linked to this truth is a final lesson—we must guard against the terrible temptation to do something simply because it is popular and expedient. Had Ahab and the people of Israel been less concerned with what others were doing, and more concerned with what God wanted them to do, they could have spared themselves untold misery and woe.

Ahab and his generation have long since passed off history's stage, but the snares which entangled them are ready to trap us, too. If we are to stand in this age of apostasy we must be watchful and prayerful so that we recognize these potential snares and elude their grasp.

2

An Age of Contempt for God's Word

In his days Hiel of Bethel built Jericho. He laid its foundation with Abiram his firstborn, and with his youngest son Segub he set up its gates, according to the word of the LORD, which He had spoken through Joshua the son of Nun.

1 Kings 16:34

After describing the idolatry Ahab brought into Israel, the author includes this brief note about Hiel's rebuilding of the walls of Jericho. Only Hiel is mentioned in connection with this project, but we can rest assured that Ahab was deeply involved. The words 'in his days' are the author's way of telling us that the king of Israel was the one responsible for creating the kind of climate and atmosphere in which such a project could take place.

On the face of things, a note about a man engaging in such a project seems harmless enough. The city of Jericho was strategically located in the south-eastern corner of the kingdom of Israel. Any enemy approaching from that direction would have to go past Jericho before he could get to the capital city of Samaria. Any king would therefore want to do exactly what Ahab commissioned Hiel to do.

But Jericho was no ordinary city. This city occupied a tremendously significant place in Israel's history. It was the first city the people of Israel encountered when they began their conquest of the land of Canaan, and at that time it was an impregnable stronghold with massive walls. As the Israelites gazed upon those ramparts their hearts must have dropped. How would they ever be able to scale the walls and take the city? Some probably began to think that the whole idea of conquering Canaan was an enormous mistake. The task appeared to be too great, and even if it could be accomplished, the cost seemed certain to be too high.

In the midst of such musings came a word from the leader of Israel, Joshua. He said the people were not even to attempt scaling those imposing walls, but instead were simply to march around Jericho once each day for six days. On the seventh day they were to march around it seven times. When the seventh trip around the city was complete, the priests were to blow their trumpets and the people were to shout. Then the walls of

Jericho, Joshua said, would come crashing down! Where did Joshua get such an apparently preposterous notion? From God himself! Many of the people of Israel probably thought this was the most ludicrous thing they had ever heard, but they had been given a leader in Joshua and it was up to them to follow him. So follow they did. They marched and marched, and at the precise moment they shouted the walls of Jericho tumbled to the ground!

Why did God choose this particular way for the people to conquer Jericho? All the other cities the people of Israel came up against were conquered through conventional methods of warfare. Why was Jericho singled out for special treatment? The answer is that God wanted Jericho to proclaim forever certain truths about himself and the people he had chosen.

Firstly, he wanted those walls to tell people about the truth of his judgement upon sin. The Canaanites who lived in that city were completely given over to the most reprehensible sins imaginable. They lived without regard to the true God and trusted in their own strength and wisdom.

Secondly, God wanted those walls to proclaim the truth of his grace. The people of Israel did absolutely nothing to make those walls fall; they supplied not even an ounce of the strength needed to topple them. All they did was to trust the promise God had given them through Joshua. Because Jericho stood at the entrance into the land of Canaan, it represented, in a sense, the whole land which was a gift of God's grace to his people.

In the fallen walls of Jericho, then, we have a visible testimony to the central truths of the gospel—sinful man stands under the judgement of God; man's wisdom and strength are insufficient to circumvent it; and the promises of God can only be received by those who trust his grace.

Because God inscribed these truths on the fallen walls of

Jericho, we should not be surprised to learn that these walls were never to be rebuilt (*Josh.* 6:26). Nothing was to erase the testimony these walls gave to God's judgement on man's sinfulness and to the necessity of relying solely upon God's grace. The message of those walls is powerfully clear—those who attempt to live on the basis of their own merits will be destroyed, while those who live by faith in the grace of God will be blessed. These are the same two principles that have been in conflict ever since sin entered this world.

After Joshua's death the people of Israel were ruled over by various judges. Some of these did much to strengthen Israel militarily, but not one of them attempted to rebuild the walls of Jericho. After the time of the judges, Israel was ruled over by kings. The first king, Saul, was evil in many ways, but he did not attempt to rebuild those walls. Then came David and Solomon, who did more to strengthen Israel than any other kings, but they did not touch those walls! When the kingdom was divided into two nations, Israel and Judah, Jericho fell within the boundaries of Israel. But none of the first six kings of Israel did anything to rebuild the city's walls.

Then came Ahab! And for the first time since the Lord said those walls were not to be rebuilt and the message of Jericho was not to be erased, the work was undertaken! Why would Ahab do such a thing? Why would he commission Hiel to do what all his predecessors had refused to do? Was he facing a military threat that made the fortification of Jericho necessary? No. As theocratic king of Israel, the one who ruled on behalf of God and as God's representative, Ahab should have known that the security of Israel did not rest in her military strength but in her God. The reason Ahab and Hiel undertook this project was because of the utter disdain and contempt they felt for the clear Word of God!

By undertaking this project, Ahab and Hiel were, in effect,

12

trying to take the land of Canaan back for those who lived on the basis of human merit. They were insisting that the land of Canaan proclaim the honour of human works rather than the honour of God's grace! God had made Canaan part of the pathway of his grace that led from Eden to Bethlehem. Ahab and Hiel wanted to take it out of that pathway of grace and put it back on the pathway of Cain and the tower builders of Babel. We can be certain that Ahab and Hiel knew about the commandment of God concerning Jericho, and we can also be sure that they had no trouble in coming up with rationalizations for why that command could be ignored. Maybe they simply said: 'Times and circumstances have changed.' Perhaps they drove a wedge between God's Word and Joshua's word and maintained that Joshua, not God, had commanded the walls should never be rebuilt. One thing is clear, wicked men are never at a loss when it comes to skirting the Word of God and justifying their wickedness.

So how did Ahab and Hiel fare in their project? The Bible tells us that Hiel's firstborn son, Abiram, died when Hiel laid the foundation for the walls; and his youngest son, Segub, died when he set up its gates. When he commenced the work Hiel lost a son. When he finished the work Hiel lost another son. And this is exactly what God had said would happen to anyone who attempted to rebuild the walls of Jericho: 'Cursed be the man before the LORD who rises up and builds this city Jericho; he shall lay its foundation with his firstborn, and with his youngest he shall set up its gates' (*Josh.* 6:26). The Word of God was minutely fulfilled! Ahab and Hiel attempted to mute the Word of God, but they only made it thunder even more loudly! Be sure about this—God's Word cannot be destroyed, it can only be confirmed.

But did Hiel not win after all? Even though he lost his sons in the process he still built the walls of Jericho, and did that not wipe out the message God wanted those walls to proclaim? Not really. God's message of judgement on man's sin and the necessity of living by grace was simply transferred to other stones—the stones marking the graves of Hiel's sons. Anyone looking at Jericho's new walls would be reminded of the tombs of those two sons and the message they conveyed. M. B. Van't Veer puts it like this: 'Above Jericho's ruins God's finger had written: "Received only through the power of faith as a gift of grace." But above the restored walls of this city the hand of God wrote: "Cursed be anyone who refuses to live by grace through faith alone."' [2]

Why did the author of this book include this verse about the rebuilding of Jericho's walls? After all, we hear nothing more about Hiel throughout the rest of Scripture. The reason was that in a single verse, as with a single stroke of the brush, the author paints for his readers a picture of how desperate were the times in which Elijah had to prophesy. Now we see how far into sin Ahab and the nation had gone. Not only was the worship of Baal being promoted and practised, but the Word of God was treated with scorn and contempt.

The lessons from this one verse are immense and profound. Our own day is one in which contempt for the Word of God is widespread and growing. How should those who love the Lord respond to this epidemic of disdain for the Word of God? We should certainly feel a sense of burden and sadness that men are capable of treating the Word of God in such a way, but at the same time we should feel joy and gladness because we know that the Word of God will never be destroyed but only confirmed. And we should pray that God will give us grace to do in our apostate age as Elijah did in his—to stand faithfully for God.

2   M.B. Van't Veer, *My God is Yahweh*, Paideia Press, St. Catherine's, Ontario, Canada, 1980, p. 24.

3

The Appearance
of Elijah

And Elijah the Tishbite, of the inhabitants of Gilead, said to Ahab, 'As the LORD God of Israel lives, before whom I stand, there shall not be dew nor rain these years, except at my word.'

1 Kings 17:1

E vil times demand godly men. Never had the nation of Israel faced a more evil time than under the reign of Ahab and his wife Jezebel. The worship of the nature god, Baal, flourished, and the Word of God was increasingly treated with contempt and disdain.

Thank God that the time of Ahab and Jezebel was also the time of the prophet Elijah. He was the godly man for this evil hour. As the great commentator, Matthew Henry, put it: 'Never was Israel so blessed with a good prophet as when it was so plagued with a bad king.'[3] The text of 1 Kings 17:1 tells us how Elijah abruptly strode into the king's court one day, announced a drought, strode out, and disappeared. What can we learn from this sudden appearance?

This would be nothing other than a graphic piece of history were it not for the fact that we who belong to God find ourselves in a time which is very similar to Elijah's. Our society, like his, is awash with the worship of false gods and is becoming increasingly hostile to the worship of the true God and the teachings of his Word. How are we to confront an age such as this? Many would argue that we are not to confront our society with the claims of God but must simply concede the whole thing to Baal and keep our religious beliefs to ourselves. A lot of 'Christians' today seem to be of this mind. As far as they are concerned, religion is something that takes place on Sunday at church and it should be kept there. Any talk of bringing religious beliefs to bear upon daily life and into the market-place makes them nervous.

Others recognize that this is God's world, and even though it is lost in sin he is still its Creator and Ruler. When society seeks to boot him out of his own world, it is part of the Christian's responsibility to speak up for God and to make his claims

---

3 Matthew Henry, *Matthew Henry's Commentary*, Volume II, Fleming
   H. Revell Company, n.d., p. 664.

known. But this is difficult and demanding work. It invites scorn, ridicule and hardship. How is it possible for us to stand for God? We can find many of the answers to that question in the remarkable figure of Elijah, and a study of his message, life and times should drive us to cultivate at the heart of our lives the same qualities that fuelled the prophet Elijah and drove him into Ahab's presence.

The principal characteristic of Elijah's confrontation with Ahab is that he approached the king with the deep conviction of the rightness of his position. We only have to look at the name 'Elijah' to find evidence of this conviction. The name means 'My God is Jahweh'. (We would say: 'My God is Jehovah'). Perhaps the court of Ahab enjoyed a good chuckle over this strange episode. Here was this rough-hewn country boy having the audacity to predict a drought. Everyone knew Baal was in control of rainfall and he would never let such a thing happen!

Ahab himself may have pretended to be unperturbed by the whole incident, but he must have been churning on the inside. When Ahab heard the name 'Elijah'(and we can be confident the prophet made sure he heard it) he knew his attempt to synthesize the worship of Baal with the worship of God was being challenged. That name 'Elijah' was a mighty declaration that God would not share his throne or his people with another. That name made clear that there was no room for negotiation or equivocation, that God and God alone is worthy of worship.

How did Elijah get his name? Some think he chose it when he decided to confront Ahab. Others think his parents gave it to him. There is no way to determine which of these theories is correct. I prefer the latter option. I like to visualize Elijah having godly parents who were deeply grieved and troubled by the steady encroachment of idolatry into Israel. (Perhaps the reason Elijah is said to have come from 'the inhabitants of Gilead' is that his parents were forced to flee to this neighbouring country because of the increasing pressure put on those Israelites who maintained faithfulness to God.) When their son was born they decided to name him 'Elijah' as a protest against the idolatry that had taken over Israel, as a declaration of their own continuing commitment to the God of Israel, and as a prayer that their son would never stray from faithfulness to that God. If this were indeed the case, those of us who are Christian parents can certainly identify with it. We also feel the pressure of rearing children in an idolatrous age. It is not necessary for us to name our sons 'Elijah', but it must be our desire to see each of our children look all the idols of this age in the face and say: 'My God is Jehovah.'

What must we do to produce children who unashamedly take such a stand for the true and living God? We must set the example for them by demonstrating an iron-like commitment to God ourselves. In other words, if we want our children to repudiate the false gods of this age, we must repudiate them ourselves. We must not make the mistake of thinking, as Ahab did, that we can have false gods if we simply acknowledge the true God. We must resist any temptation to create a synthesis of our own between the God of the Bible and some other god such as pleasure, possessions, comfort or fame.

Of course, there is much more to do. We must certainly teach the Word of God to our children in a careful, continual, diligent and detailed manner. We must teach them at home and make sure they are in the house of God for the teaching and preaching of God's Word. We must also earnestly pray for them and commit them to the grace of God. But, most of all, we must make sure that our praying and teaching flow from a life that decisively says: 'My God is Jehovah.'

When Elijah went in to confront Ahab he was armed with

more than the rock-ribbed conviction expressed by his name. He also had implicit faith in the truth of God's Word. Have you ever wondered how he arrived at this idea that God was going to send a drought upon Israel? Is this just something he picked out of mid-air, persuaded himself was going to take place, and then announced it to Ahab? Many Christians think this is what faith is. Pick something out that you want to be true, believe it will become true, and, presto, it happens!

Elijah's faith rested on firmer ground. He knew from the writings of Moses that God had already spoken about what would happen if the people of Israel turned aside from him to worship other gods: 'Take heed to yourselves, lest your heart be deceived, and you turn aside and serve other gods and worship them, "lest the LORD'S anger be aroused against you, and He shut up the heavens so that there be no rain, . . . ' (*Deut.* 11:16-17). On the basis of that clear and distinct promise, Elijah began, according to James 5:17, to pray earnestly 'that it would not rain'. Why pray for something God has already promised to do? There are two answers. First, God has told us to pray for what he has promised. Second, if we pray for what God has promised we can rest assured our prayer will be answered.

Now we are in position to see what true faith is as well as what it is to pray in faith. Faith is simply believing what God has revealed in his Word. Paul says: 'faith comes by hearing, and hearing by the word of God' (*Rom.* 10:17). And praying in faith means laying hold of the promises of God's Word, pleading them before God, and saying to God: 'do as You have said' (*2 Sam.* 7:25).

In the course of his praying, Elijah became convinced that the time was right to appear before Ahab. He knew God had promised to send a drought on Israel for her idolatry, but how did he know when God would send it? A little later we learn that the drought lasted about three years after Elijah made his announcement to Ahab (*1 Kings* 18:1). But in the New Testament we find Jesus saying the drought of Elijah's time lasted three-and-a-half years (*Luke* 4:25). How are we to explain this discrepancy? The answer is the drought actually started six months before Elijah made his appearance to Ahab! As Elijah saw the early months of this drought begin to unfold he became convinced God had heard his prayers and was already fulfilling his promise.

So Elijah went to Ahab. In addition to going with deep conviction and full assurance of faith, he went with a clear and distinct message. When we look closely at Elijah's message we see immediately that it was delivered in the name not of a god who consisted only of wood or stone, but in the name of the God who lives. It was, in fact, God's own message. It was not something Elijah dreamed up on his own. Elijah made this clear by referring to himself as one standing before the Lord (verse 1). The picture here is of a servant who stands before his master waiting to hear his command. Ahab thought Elijah was the one responsible for this message (verse 17), but he was dealing not with a mere human prophet but with the eternal God himself!

And the message Elijah brought was clear in its open and direct challenge to Ahab's false god. Baal was supposed to be in control of rainfall, but Elijah's message launched a frontal assault on that claim. Elijah declared that there would be absolutely no rain in Israel until he, the servant of the true God, said so. In this way, the impotence of Baal would be clearly demonstrated before the whole nation.

Do we have anything of the mind and spirit of Elijah about us? Can we say we are totally convinced of the rightness of our position? Can we say we are fully persuaded of the truth of God's Word? When we do make the claims of God known to someone, are we proclaiming it in an authoritative way that shows the failures of the false gods of our day?

Elijah was indeed a unique man, a man prepared by God for that specific hour. We can never be all that he was, but we can be some of what he was. May God help us to have something of his spirit. What could God do with Christians who had just a small measure of the qualities Elijah possessed?

4

Elijah Goes to Cherith and Zarephath

Then the word of the LORD came to him, saying, 'Get away from here and turn eastward, and hide by the Brook Cherith, which flows into the Jordan. And it will be that you shall drink from the brook, and I have commanded the ravens to feed you there.' So he went and did according to the word of the LORD, for he went and stayed by the Brook Cherith, which flows into the Jordan. The ravens brought him bread and meat in the morning, and bread and meat in the evening; and he drank from the brook. And it happened after a while that the brook dried up, because there had been no rain in the land. Then the word of the LORD came to him, saying, 'Arise, go to Zarephath, which belongs to Sidon, and dwell there. See, I have commanded a widow there to provide for you.'

1 Kings 17:2–9

T he people of Israel stood in a special covenant relationship to God. They were to live the whole of their
lives under the authority of the Word of God. When
King Ahab came to the throne, he promoted a sinister con-
cept. He separated one part of Israel's life from the Word of
God. He said the forces of nature were gods themselves and he
placed these alongside the true God. Once we say some part of
our lives does not come under the authority of God's Word we
set ourselves up for calamity.

It did not take long for the calamity to come upon Israel.
The prophet Elijah burst into Ahab's court one day to say
there would be no rain or dew until he, Elijah, said so. With
that brief word, the prophet walked out and disappeared. The
verses before us tell us that the time Elijah was hidden from
view fell into two phases. The first phase was spent in total
isolation at the Brook Cherith. The second phase was spent at
a widow's house in Zarephath.

These two episodes are usually taken to mean that God will
find some way to provide for his people even in times of
severe distress and deprivation. This interpretation is very
appealing in times of recession and unemployment. Of course,
the Bible does urge the children of God to pray for their daily
bread (*Luke* 11:3) and to trust the Lord to supply their needs
(*Phil.* 4:19), but that is not the point of this part of the story of
Elijah.

The key to unlocking the meaning of Elijah hiding at
Cherith and Zarephath is to equate Elijah with the Word of
God. When Elijah stood before Ahab and said there would be
no dew or rain 'except at my word', we should see the Word of
God converging and coinciding with the prophet himself.
From that moment, the Word of God became for all practical
purposes totally embodied in and identified with the prophet.
Cherith and Zarephath, then, are not merely interesting side-

lights in the life of the prophet, or proofs that God will provide for his people, but are conveyors of vital lessons about the Word of God. Once we see these lessons, our confidence in God's Word grows by leaps and bounds.

Such confidence is sorely needed by many Christians who are constantly filled with doubt and anxiety about God's Word. As Uzza feared the ark of the covenant toppling to the ground, many seem to fear the Word of God being discredited and the cause of God failing. Ours is a day in which Christians seem to think the Bible has to correspond to modern teachings or it cannot be believed. We tend to accept such teachings at face value and never get around to asking if it just might be possible that the Bible could be right and the modern teachings wrong.

Let us follow Elijah to Cherith and Zarephath to see what we can learn about the Word of God.

1.   *The Calamity of the Secluded Word.*
When we read that Elijah was commanded to hide at Cherith we are immediately inclined to think God was protecting him from Ahab. The truth is that Elijah was hidden not for his own sake but for Israel's. By hiding Elijah, the Lord was depriving his people of the Word of God and showing them they were under his wrath and sore displeasure.

We tend to associate God's sending judgement with an immediate outburst of catastrophe, but the first thing God usually does is simply to withhold his blessings, and there is no greater blessing than the hearing of the Word of God! The people of Israel were the most blessed of all nations because they had been given the Word of God. Had they listened to it and obeyed it they would have continued to be blessed, but they turned aside and embraced Baal. Because they had refused to listen to that Word, God said, in effect, 'You won't have my Word to listen to!'

There was in the kingdom, then, a double famine—the physical famine that resulted from the drought and the spiritual famine that resulted from not hearing the Word of God. Years later, the prophet Amos predicted another spiritual famine for the nation of Israel (*Amos* 8:11-12). Are we seeing this kind of judgement today? Has the Word of God been withdrawn from us? Is there a famine of the Word? It would not seem so. After all, the land is dotted with churches and there seems to be no shortage of preachers. But the fact that we are well stocked with churches and preachers is no guarantee that the Word of God is being preached. Even in churches which profess to believe the Bible one can hear very little of God's Word. There are all kinds of sermons on living successfully and coping with life's problems and difficulties, but there is precious little preaching on the depth of man's sin, the reality of judgement before a holy God, the necessity of God's saving grace, and the sufficiency of Christ's death on the cross. There is, I believe, much that is interesting and entertaining in preaching today but little to induce deep conviction and changed lives.

2. *The Certainty of the Sustained Word.*

When we learn that God's Word was at this time equated with the prophet Elijah, we might be excused for thinking it was hanging by a perilous thread indeed. What if Ahab found Elijah and put him to death? What if Elijah were unable to survive the drought he himself had predicted? If the cause of God were to rest with this solitary prophet, it would seem to be teetering on the verge of extinction.

The fact that the Lord preserved Elijah while he was hiding at the brook teaches us that God will always sustain his Word. Even though his cause may appear to be on the verge of total collapse, we may rest assured it will never fail. Even if the number of his faithful people shrinks to one, that believer will be preserved and sustained! No matter how the gates of hell rage against it, the cause of God will never perish. In order to preserve his faithful messenger, the Lord went so far as to command ravens to feed Elijah while he was hiding at the brook. Ravens are, of course, birds of prey, and yet they were commanded to bring Elijah food. In other words, they were commanded to do the very thing their nature precluded them from doing! The Word of God effectively overruled their basic nature!

What truth can we draw from this? Namely this: that the Lord can use even those who are by nature violently opposed to his Word to serve that very Word. The Bible tells us he can even use the wrath of man to praise him (*Ps.* 76:10). As Hiel found in his rebuilding of the walls of Jericho, the Word of God cannot be silenced; and the more we try to silence it the louder it speaks. Many today have, for example, tried to silence what the Bible has to say about sexual immorality. Have they in any way succeeded? No. The harder they try to flaunt the standards of biblical morality the greater the price they pay in their own bodies.

Elijah must have marvelled day after day as he saw the ravens swooping down toward him to lay food gently in his out-stretched hand. Baal was supposedly the god of nature and here God was demonstrating his authority over nature. If Elijah ever entertained any doubts about the final outcome of this battle against Baal, he must have seen them all fly away with the flapping of those ravens' wings.

It was not long until the brook dried up and the Lord commanded Elijah to go to Zarephath. Could God not have continued to provide for Elijah at Cherith? Of course! The God who at one time made enough water come out of a rock to quench the thirst of a multitude could certainly have provided water for one prophet. The drying of the brook was God's way of letting Elijah know it was time for him to go to the next phase of his hiding, a phase which shows us a third aspect of the Word of God.

3. *The Consolation of the Serving Word.*

The reason God moved Elijah from Cherith to Zarephath is that Cherith was not a complete revelation of the truth about God's Word. Cherith proclaimed the truth that God will sustain his Word, but Zarephath proclaims the truth that God will actively use his Word. Elijah was in complete isolation while he was at Cherith, but at Zarephath there was a widow who needed the ministry of the Word.

We ought to thank God for the truth of Cherith—God will sustain his Word against all odds—but we must not allow ourselves to develop a Cherith mentality. The reality of God sustaining his Word must not be taken to mean we can sit back in idleness. God is not only interested in preserving his Word but in using it. The Word of God is, according to the author of Hebrews, a living, powerful, active Word (*Heb.* 4:12), and we may rest assured that it is at work accomplishing God's purposes. Even though the Word was hidden from Israel at this time it was not inactive, and we can be confident that even in those times when God appears to be doing nothing, his Word is secretly at work.

4. *The Judgement of Those Who Possess the Word.*

Zarephath also lays another truth before us. The widow to whom Elijah was sent was a Gentile. The sending of Elijah to her was a dramatic representation of the truth that no one has a monopoly on God. He is sovereign and works when he will and with whom he will. The people of Israel had great difficulty with this. They took their covenant relationship with

God to mean that he was their exclusive property. They never seemed to grasp that their call to a special relationship with God was not a call to privileged status but to obedient living. By sending Elijah to Zarephath, God was giving his people notice that their continued rejection of his Word would result in their being replaced by another people. This is, in fact, what finally happened. When the Jews decisively rejected Jesus, God began to engraft into his covenant a new Israel made up of all those who receive Christ.

It is true, of course, that the people of Israel did not know at this time that Elijah was in Zarephath, and did not realize, therefore, the spiritual lessons this conveyed. But the account of Elijah's going to Zarephath did enter into the Scriptures as a testimony to future generations of what would happen to those who take God's Word lightly.

Cherith and Zarephath are not just curious places to look for on a map of Bible times. They represent vital principles for each and every one of us. They tell us that if we take the Word of God lightly, we invite God to judge us by removing the preaching and teaching of it. They tell us not to be discouraged by this age of doubt and scepticism but to rest in the assurance that God's Word will never fail. They tell us that God's Word will not only be sustained but will be actively at work achieving his purpose.

5

Elijah at the
Widow's House

Then the word of the LORD came to him, saying, 'Arise, go to Zarephath, which belongs to Sidon, and dwell there. See, I have commanded a widow there to provide for you.' So he arose and went to Zarephath. And when he came to the gate of the city, indeed a widow was there gathering sticks. And he called to her and said, 'Please bring me a little water in a cup, that I may drink.' As she was going to get it, he called to her and said, 'Please bring me a morsel of bread in your hand.' Then she said, 'As the LORD your God lives, I do not have bread, only a handful of flour in a bin, and a little oil in a jar; and see, I am gathering a couple of sticks that I may go in and prepare it for myself and my son, that we may eat it, and die.' And Elijah said to her, 'Do not fear; go and do as you have said, but make me a small cake from it first, and bring it to me; and afterward make some for yourself and your son. For thus says the LORD God of Israel: "The bin of flour shall not be used up, nor shall the jar of oil run dry until the day the LORD sends rain on the earth."' So she went away and did according to the word of Elijah; and she and he and her household ate for many days. The bin of flour was not used up, nor did the jar of oil run dry, according to the word of the LORD which He spoke by Elijah.

1 Kings 17:8–16

The comings and goings of a prophet in ancient Israel probably seem dull fare to most people. Even Christians seem more interested in the itineraries of politicians, athletes, movie stars and rock singers than in the travels of Elijah. Why should we concern ourselves with Elijah going to a widow's house in Zarephath?

The answer is that Elijah was more than just a prophet. He was at this moment in Israel's history the very embodiment of the Word of God. When we look, therefore, at what he did and where he went, we should ask ourselves what these things teach us about the Word of God. Once we realize this, the story of Elijah leaps over the barriers of time and becomes immensely interesting and relevant because the Word of God is a major component in the Christian's life. No true Christian can ever say he is not interested in the Word of God. That Word is to the Christian what food is to the body, what a road map is to the traveller, and what medicine is to the sick. It is absolutely indispensable to the Christian. Anyone who says he is not interested in the Word of God is openly proclaiming he is not a child of God.

We can learn much about the Word of God from following Elijah to the widow's house in Zarephath. First, we see the Word of God comes to us with sovereign authority. To appreciate the significance of this we only have to glance at a map. Zarephath was not located in Israel's territory at all. It was in Phoenicia. Have you ever wondered why God sent Elijah to such a far-flung place?

As we have already seen, God could have sustained Elijah forever at the brook at Cherith. There was no need or physical reason why Elijah should travel to Zarephath. Nor was the move to provide Elijah with some human companionship. If that were the case, why did God not send Elijah to one of the widows in Israel (*Luke* 4:25-26)? Some would answer that

Elijah might have been discovered if he stayed in Israel, but God was just as capable of protecting the prophet right under Ahab's nose as he was in a far-off land. Neither was the journey necessary because the widow was seeking knowledge of the true God. When Elijah began talking to the woman she undoubtedly recognized him as being an Israelite and she referred to his God (verse 12), but in so doing she made it clear that his God was not her God. Although the Lord said that he had 'commanded' a widow in Zarephath to care for Elijah (verse 9), how could he do so if she did not even own him as her God? The only answer is that the Lord had chosen her before she was even aware of it. She was selected to serve as a hostess to the Word of God before she ever chose to. It was all due to God's sovereign grace at work in her life.

This is not to say that God exercises his sovereignty without any rhyme or reason. It must not be lost on us that Phoenicia was the home of that arch-promoter of the worship of Baal— Jezebel. In choosing this woman to host his prophet and to receive his blessings the Lord was demonstrating his sovereign power over Baal. While the impotence of Baal was being fully demonstrated in the land of God, the power of God was being fully demonstrated in the land of Baal.

Christians are in acute need of this truth of the sovereignty of the Word. We live in a day of competing messages. As we survey the scene it becomes easy for us to believe that all kinds of false messages are flourishing and our own message seems to be pitifully weak and ineffective. Thank God, the whole story is not apparent by human observation. The Word of God is powerful and effective. We can preach it with the utmost confidence that it will do its work. We do not have to apologize for it, embellish it or change it because we have God's own promise that just as 'the rain comes down, and the snow from heaven, and do not return there, but water the earth, and make it bring forth and bud, that it may give seed to the sower and bread to the eater, so shall My word be that goes forth from My mouth; it shall not return to Me void, but it shall accomplish what I please, and it shall prosper in the thing for which I sent it' (*Isa.* 55:10–11).

Elijah's visit to the widow also shows us that the Word of God demands our all. When Elijah came upon this widow he first asked her for a drink of water. This may have been his way of determining whether this woman was indeed the one to whom the Lord was sending him. It is probable that the drought in Israel was also affecting the surrounding countries. Her willingness to give away water at such a time would be a clear indication that she was the one whom the Lord had selected. As soon as the woman turned to her house to get the water, Elijah called to her and asked her to bring him some food also.

It was now that the woman poured out her wretched story. All she had left in the house was a handful of flour and a little oil. She was gathering wood to make a fire so she could bake a little cake for her son and herself. They were going to eat that cake and then wait to die! Had you and I been there to overhear this exchange between Elijah and the woman, we would fully expect him to say something like this: 'I'm very sorry, madam. I had no idea you were in such desperate straits. Forgive me for asking.' And then we would expect to see him move on.

Nothing like that happened. Instead, Elijah says what seems to be the most unkind, callous thing possible. Essentially, he responded to the woman's plight by saying: 'Go ahead and make the cake and give it to me!' What lesson are we to draw from this? Are we to conclude that Elijah was a selfish, unfeeling, insensitive brute, or is there something else here? We must remember again to equate Elijah with the Word of God. His demand, therefore, was the demand of the Word of God upon this woman. This element of the story must not be used, then, as a basis for individual preachers satisfying their desires by demanding that everyone give everything they possess! Amazingly, this has been the way some preachers have used this passage, but they have no right to make such demands.

The Word of God, however, does have the right to demand our all, even as it did with this woman. But, thank God, the Word of God always couples its demands with a promise. Elijah had no sooner told this woman to use the last bit of meal and oil for him than he assured the woman that the barrel would never be emptied and the oil would never run out. Put yourself in the shoes of this poor, famished woman. She was faced at that moment with an awesome choice. She was being asked to give up something she could see and touch but which was almost at an end for something she could not yet see or touch but was promised to last through the drought.

What would she do? What would you do? Somehow, she heard the Word of God sounding in the words of Elijah. The power of that Word worked faith in her heart, she willingly did as Elijah commanded, and received the promise he had given. Notice, however, that she actually had to do something. She was not allowed to get by with merely telling Elijah that she believed in her heart everything he was saying. She actually had to act upon that. She could have nodded her agreement endlessly, but she could only prove her faith by scraping the last handful of meal out of that barrel, pouring out that last precious drop of oil from the jar, and making Elijah that cake.

Has it occurred to you that this is nothing less than a miniature picture of the gospel of Jesus Christ? The gospel confronts you with the same demand: namely, to give your all. Oh, it seems like this is so very much, but in reality our all is like the widow's barrel and oil—temporary and perishing.

The gospel also confronts us with a promise. Just as Elijah said 'Do not fear' to this woman, so the gospel says 'Do not fear' to us. It assures us that the giving of our all will result in far greater blessing than we can conceive. In short it, like Elijah, calls us to give up what is temporal and perishing for that which is permanent and incorruptible. But the gospel tells us that it is not enough simply to say that we believe. As Elijah insisted the widow demonstrate her faith by acting upon the Word she had heard, so the gospel insists we demonstrate our faith by living changed lives.

In embracing the word of Elijah the woman was making faith in God the primary concern of her life and her own comfort secondary. The people of Israel had been called to do the very same thing, but they had inverted their priorities. Instead of living on the basis of faith in the Word of God they had embraced Baal as a means of securing their own comfort. God used this obscure Gentile widow in Zarephath to demonstrate how his people were supposed to be living.

What will it be with you? Will you join this little known woman of Zarephath and say: 'Man shall not live by bread alone, but by every word that proceeds from the mouth of God' (*Matt.* 4:4)? Or will you join the multitudes of Israel who scorned the demands of God's Word and lived only for the moment?

6

When God Seems
to Fail

*Now it happened after these things that the son of the woman who owned
the house became sick. And his sickness was so serious that there was no
breath left in him. So she said to Elijah, 'What have I to do with you, O
man of God? Have you come to me to bring my sin to remembrance, and
to kill my son?' And he said to her, 'Give me your son.' So he took him
out of her arms and carried him to the upper room where he was staying,
and laid him on his own bed. Then he cried out to the LORD and said,
'O LORD my God, have You also brought tragedy on the widow with
whom I lodge, by killing her son?' And he stretched himself out on the
child three times, and cried out to the LORD and said, 'O LORD my
God, I pray, let this child's soul come back to him!' Then the LORD heard
the voice of Elijah'; and the soul of the child came back to him, and he
revived. And Elijah took the child and brought him down from the upper
room into the house, and gave him to his mother. And Elijah said, 'See,
your son lives!' Then the woman said to Elijah, 'Now by this I know that
you are a man of God, and that the word of the LORD in your mouth is
the truth.'*

1 Kings 17:17–24

When Elijah first appeared at the widow's house in Zarephath, she and her son were facing death. Their food supply had dwindled to the point where there was only enough meal and oil to make a small cake, and the widow had absolutely no hope of being able to secure any more supplies. So she and her son were going to eat the cake and simply wait for the slow, agonizing death of starvation. All of that changed when Elijah showed up. He gave the widow a promise from God himself, a promise that drew them back from the dark abyss of death and brought back the joy of living. Implicit in that promise was the guarantee that the widow and her son would continue to live as long as the drought lasted.

This passage, then, comes as a terrible shock to us because it tells of the death of the widow's son. And the shock we feel cannot compare to the shock the widow and Elijah must have felt. There was still flour in the barrel and oil in the jar, but one of those for whom the promise was given had died.

This sudden, tragic development thrust both the widow and the prophet into a great dilemma. Why would God take the life of one he had seemingly promised to sustain? Was the Word of God so unreliable? Was God nothing more than a cruel tyrant who enjoyed playing games with people? Had he just raised their hopes so he could take pleasure in dashing them to the ground? Or was God unable to fulfil his promise? Were his good intentions destroyed by a lack of power? Essentially, the human mind seems compelled to conclude that God is either malevolent or impotent.

Every child of God has spent time at the widow's house. At one time or another we have all found ourselves staring blankly into the leering face of suffering. We have all heard its taunts: 'Perhaps your God is cruel. He makes promises he has no intention of keeping. Or else he is impotent. He wants to keep his promises but can't.' What is a Christian to do when he finds himself at the widow's house? What is he to do when everything seems to go sour and the God he so fondly trusted in seems to have failed him? This episode yields two principles to sustain and guide each child of God who is befuddled by Zarephath's riddle.

1. *When God Seems to Fail—Wait and Trust (verse 18).*
When her son died the widow's world came crashing down around her. She had spoken very stoically about the prospect of her son dying when Elijah first came on the scene, perhaps because she knew she was going to die also. But now her son was dead and she was left, and the pain was almost more than she could bear. She felt her heart had been ripped out and life was not worth living.

In the searing grief and anguish of the moment, she began to assign blame for this crushing blow. First she blamed Elijah and his God: 'What have I to do with you, O man of God?' was her way of saying: 'Why have you and your God allowed this to happen to me?'

Then, as if to answer her own question, she turned the focus on herself. Perhaps she was to blame. Perhaps Elijah's God had brought this calamity because of that one terrible act of wickedness she had always felt so guilty about, that sin she had never been able to dismiss, that sin which had dogged her steps and tortured her mind. Yes, that sin must be the reason for her loss! God had sent Elijah to bring judgement upon her, and that one sin was so great God had decided to lift her up with a miracle before dashing her to the earth with this catastrophe.

It is easy to identify with the widow. Her reaction is so typical of all of us. When some calamity or trial befalls us we immediately feel we have to find a way to explain it, and, like her, we find it easy to blame God, ourselves, or both. Of course, we can always easily find plenty of reasons to blame ourselves for catastrophes, and when we do we forget all about the grace of God. But when we get angry with God, it is usually a matter of wanting to hold him accountable for things he has never promised. We get angry at him if one of our loved ones gets sick or dies, but God has nowhere promised our loved ones would never get sick or die. In fact, the Bible tells us just the opposite. It constantly tells us that this life is a realm of sin with all its attendant woes, and the children of God will never be free from these things until that day in heaven when God wipes all the tears away from our eyes.

In the case of the widow, however, the Lord had given her the implicit promise that she and her son would be spared until the famine was over. What are we to say about this? Simply this—do not be too quick to judge God on the basis of outward appearances. It may appear that he has failed to keep his promises, but in reality he never fails. We may rest assured that when he seems to fail, it is just that—seeming failure. He fails in our limited way of seeing things, but he never truly fails to keep a promise. When he appears to fail it is only because he has a greater purpose in mind.

With the widow and her son, God did not fail at all. The son lived. But in seeming to fail God accomplished two great things. Firstly, he brought the woman to a higher plane of trust than she ever had before. She came away from this experience saying: 'Now by this I know that you are a man of God, and that the word of the LORD in your mouth is the truth' (verse 24). Secondly, by seeming to fail God gave Elijah a powerful object lesson. For all practical purposes the nation of Israel was dead, but there was no need for Elijah to despair because he received through the widow's son first-hand evidence that God can raise the dead! When the Lord finally said to Elijah: 'Go, present yourself to Ahab' (18:1), Elijah went in full confidence of the power of the omnipotent God.

2.   *When God Seems to Fail—Pray (verses 19-22).*
It is obvious that Elijah was deeply troubled and bewildered by the boy's death—but there was a significant difference between him and the widow. While she considered the situation to be hopeless and irreversible, he did not. Elijah had faith in the promise of God. He knew the promise to multiply the widow's flour and oil carried with it the promise that their lives would be preserved through the drought.

As far as Elijah was concerned, the fact that the boy was dead did not nullify the promise. Elijah knew God would somehow keep his promise even though the boy had died. This is much the same situation that Abraham found himself in. The Lord had promised to give him descendants through his son, Isaac, but before Isaac had any offspring the Lord commanded Abraham to take him up Mount Moriah and offer him as a sacrifice. Abraham's mind must have been in a whirl! How could he reconcile God's promise to give him descendants through Isaac with this command to sacrifice Isaac? The author of Hebrews tells us how Abraham was able to reconcile these things: 'By faith Abraham, when he was tested, offered up Isaac, and he who had received the promises offered up his only begotten son . . . accounting that God was able to raise him up, even from the dead' (*Heb.* 11:17, 19). In other words, when Abraham took Isaac up that mountain to sacrifice him, he did so with the knowledge that Isaac would survive the ordeal. Abraham knew that even if he had to carry out the sacrifice his son would be raised up. Such was his faith in the promise of God.

Faith, therefore, is not merely believing anything we want, but it is believing the promises of God. Elijah believed he had such a promise. He did not, however, take a fatalistic attitude and say: 'If God wants that boy to live he will raise him up without my involvement.' Instead, he took the boy up to his own bed and began to pray for him to be raised up. Three features of this prayer stand out:

    i.   *Elijah's prayer was fervent and intense.*

We are told that Elijah 'cried out to the Lord' (verse 20). In addition to that, Elijah also 'stretched himself out on the child' (verse 21). This, I take it, was an indication of how deeply Elijah felt about this situation. He was so moved he would have, if possible, imparted his own life into the boy.

    ii.   *Elijah's prayer pleaded the promise before God and*
        reasoned with him on the basis of it.

He said 'O LORD my God, have You also brought tragedy on the widow with whom I lodge, by killing her son?' (verse 20). Essentially, Elijah was saying: 'Lord, you can't allow this. You have made a promise to sustain this widow and her son and you must honour your promise. Your honour and glory are at stake here.' We always have great difficulty here. We constantly think that if the Lord has promised something we need not worry about praying for it, but just the opposite is true. If the Lord has promised something, we have every reason to pray for it because we know it will be given. God's promises should not be seen in a fatalistic way ('They will come true no matter what we do'), but in a living, dynamic way. In other words, when God gives a promise he not only determines a specific end will be achieved, but he also determines the means by which that end is to be attained. That is the reason why it is so important for us to pray on the basis of God's promises. Prayer is the means by which God's promises are activated and his purposes achieved. When we begin to study the great prayers of the Bible we invariably find this element of holding God to his word (*Gen.* 32:11-12; *Neh.* 1:8-11; *Dan.* 9:2-4).

iii. *Elijah's prayer demonstrated perseverance.*

The prophet was not content merely to toss a petition toward God and walk away with a shrug of the shoulders. Instead he stretched himself out on the boy three times (verse 21).

All of this should make us ask why we are not seeing more of the blessing of God upon our own lives and churches. Is it because we have no promises from God? No! It's because we have refused to tap those promises with fervent, believing, persevering prayer. If you are one of those who happens to be in the depths of despair because you feel God has failed you, remember to wait and pray. These may seem to be well-worn paths, and you may find yourself desiring some new teaching that will make things easier. But there is a reason paths are well worn. Lots of feet have trodden them! And the reason so many feet have trodden these paths is that they lead to peace.

7

The Second Meeting of
Elijah and Ahab

Now it came to pass after many days that the word of the LORD came to Elijah, in the third year, saying, 'Go, present yourself to Ahab, and I will send rain on the earth.' So Elijah went to present himself to Ahab; and there was a severe famine in Samaria. And Ahab had called Obadiah, who was in charge of his house. (Now Obadiah feared the LORD greatly. For so it was, while Jezebel massacred the prophets of the LORD, that Obadiah had taken one hundred prophets and hidden them, fifty to a cave, and had fed them with bread and water.) And Ahab had said to Obadiah, 'Go into the land to all the springs of water and to all the brooks.; perhaps we may find grass to keep the horses and mules alive, so that we will not have to kill any livestock.' So they divided the land between them to explore it; Ahab went one way by himself, and Obadiah went another way by himself. Now as Obadiah was on his way, suddenly Elijah met him; and he recognised him, and fell on his face, and said, 'Is
(continued over)

———————————

that you, my lord Elijah?' And he answered him, 'It is I. Go, tell your master, "Elijah is here." ' Then he said, 'How have I sinned, that you are delivering your servant into the hand of Ahab, to kill me?' As the LORD your God lives, there is no nation or kingdom where my master has not sent someone to hunt for you: and when they said, "He is not here," he took an oath from the kingdom or nation that they could not find you. And now you say, "Go tell your master, 'Elijah is here' "!And it shall come to pass, as soon as I am gone from you, that the Spirit of the LORD will carry you to a place I do not know; so when I go and tell Ahab, and he cannot find you, he will kill me. But I your servant have feared the LORD from my youth. Was it not reported to my lord what I did when Jezebel killed the prophets of the LORD, how I hid one hundred men of the LORD's prophets, fifty to a cave, and fed them with bread and water? And now you say, "Go, tell your master, 'Elijah is here!' " and he will kill me.' Then Elijah said, 'As the LORD of hosts lives, before whom I stand, I will surely present myself to him today.' So Obadiah went to meet Ahab, and told him; and Ahab went to meet Elijah.

1 Kings 18:1-16

———————————

At some point after Elijah disappeared Ahab launched an all-out search for him (18:10). The purpose of this search was to bring the prophet before the king and, presumably, to wring the word out of him which would end the famine that was gradually destroying Israel. As he saw his kingdom shrivelling away before his very eyes, Ahab may well have consoled himself by envisioning that shining moment when some of his soldiers would burst into his court and fling Elijah to the floor in front of him. How quickly Elijah would say the magical word to end the famine as he grovelled before Ahab and begged for his life!

It was not to be. Elijah was not found by Ahab's soldiers but simply showed up when God gave him the word. And Elijah was not brought before the king at all but demanded that the king come before him. What a strange turn of events! Ahab, as king, was accustomed to everyone serving him. He would summon whomever he wished and that person would do whatever he commanded. But here the roles are reversed. Ahab is the one who is summoned and he is told what he must do (18:19). It is clear from this passage that Elijah, not Ahab, was the one who was setting the agenda.

How are we to explain such a thing? We must not resort to some sort of psychological explanation and say the commanding, majestic figure of Elijah was what moved Ahab to answer his summons. Such an interpretation forgets that Elijah was at this time the bearer of the Word of God. So when Elijah commanded Ahab to stand before him, it was nothing less than the Word of God demanding the king's complete and total submission.

Once we see this truth, then this passage no longer appears to be a slice of ancient history with no meaning or value. Because here we have two men who represent two totally different ways of life. Ahab represents the life lived without

47

regard to the Word of God and Elijah represents the life lived in obedience to that Word, and the former has finally to bow to the latter.

This was an amazing development and it deserves careful consideration. To appreciate fully how monumental it was for Ahab to answer Elijah's summons we must look at two realities—the hard-heartedness of the one summoned by the Word of God, and the half-heartedness of the one used to do the summoning.

1. *The Hard-heartedness of Ahab, the One Summoned by Elijah.*
Ahab was hard-hearted toward the Word of God even before Elijah appeared on the scene. As the king of God's covenant people he was thoroughly versed in his nation's religious heritage. He knew, for instance, what Moses had said about the only way the nation could ensure the productivity of the land. Moses had stated it both positively and negatively. On the positive side, he said that if the people would live in obedience to God their land would yield bountifully (*Deut.* 28:1-4, 12). On the negative side, Moses said that if the people refused to obey God's commands they would bring drought upon themselves (*Deut.* 28:15-18, 22-24).

Ahab knew all of this, but because his heart was hard toward the Word of God he plunged madly ahead in leading Israel to assign control of the weather to the false god, Baal. We should not be surprised to read of such things. We know something of the nature of the human heart, and we know how easy it is to rebel against the clear teachings of God's Word. But after we read that God sent Elijah to announce the drought and that the drought came just as Elijah predicted, we might expect to find Ahab's heart softened and to see him admitting his wrong and leading the people in wholehearted repentance.

Yet the opening verses of this chapter reveal Ahab had no

intention of turning from his sin. The drought was 'severe' (*1 Kings* 18:2). There was absolutely no way to explain it in natural terms. It had to be due to God's making good the threat he had delivered through Moses. But as this chapter opens we do not find Ahab on his face before God. He could have remembered what King David did when famine came to the kingdom during his reign. David 'inquired of the Lord' (*2 Sam.* 21:1), learned the famine was due to sin, and dealt with that sin. Such thoughts seem to have been as far removed from Ahab's mind as rain clouds were from the sky.

Ahab's response to the situation, after all this time to think and reflect, was to divide the land with his steward, Obadiah, and go looking for enough grass and water to keep his horses and mules alive for a few more days! No mention is made of his making plans to help his subjects. Such was his hardness of heart that horses and mules took priority over people.

Yet, incredibly, it was this man with the heart as hard as Israel's baked earth who answers Elijah's summons and goes out to meet him. Are we to understand from this that Ahab had finally come to the end of his tether and was planning to change his ways? Not at all. Why then did he go? From the human perspective, Ahab probably went to Elijah out of hatred for the man and with the intent of seizing him or perhaps out of sheer desperation to end the drought. But from the divine perspective, this godless king was answering the summons of the Word of God. Ahab would never have willingly admitted that he was acknowledging the truth of God's Word, but it is significant that he ended up doing exactly what Elijah told him to do (verses 19-20).

Ahab did not have a monopoly on hard-heartedness toward God. There are no shortages of Ahabs in our own time. Even though the Word of God has been abundantly confirmed time after time down through the intervening centuries, there are multitudes who insist on living as though it were a myth. Sometimes Christians get discouraged by the sheer amount of hostility to God there is in this world. We may rest assured that all those who share Ahab's hard-heartedness will also share his fate. They will some day be compelled to answer the summons of the Word of God and admit it is true whether they want to or not (*Phil.* 2:9-11).

2. *The Half-heartedness of Obadiah, the One Used by Elijah to Deliver the Summons.*

Obadiah, Ahab's servant, poses a great riddle for us. On the one hand we are told he feared the Lord greatly (verse 3) and he hid a hundred prophets from Jezebel's murderous rage (verse 4). On the other hand, we cannot help but wonder how a true servant of God could be so closely linked with the likes of Ahab and Jezebel. We are further troubled by his initial reluctance to do as Elijah commanded (verse 9). Faithful but faint-hearted seems to be the best way to explain Obadiah. He was certainly a true servant of the Lord and had done much for Jehovah's cause, but he was also reluctant to do any more than what he had already done.

It is no mere coincidence that the Lord's sovereign appointment caused the paths of Elijah and Obadiah to cross. Why did he bring them together? It was so that Elijah could send Obadiah to Ahab. Elijah could have gone to Ahab himself, or he could have asked Obadiah to lead him to Ahab, but, as we have noted, Elijah wanted Ahab to answer the summons of the Word of God. Someone had to deliver that summons and Obadiah was the one the Lord had chosen for the task. He was the logical choice because he was the one servant of the Lord who enjoyed immediate access to Ahab. But it seems likely that the Lord had another purpose in all of this. Obadiah had served faithfully but secretly. By putting this burden upon him the Lord appears to have been making it clear that the time for secret discipleship was over and he must now come to the forefront of the battle.

As the one who had hidden the prophets, Obadiah was, for all practical purposes, the representative of all the remaining believers in Israel. We have with Elijah, then, the representative of the Word of God and with Obadiah the representative of the church of that day. In Elijah's command to Obadiah to go to Ahab, we see the Word of God taking hold of the people of God and pressing them into service. The Word of God can work alone, but God has chosen for it to work primarily through human instruments.

Obadiah preferred the Word to work apart from his involvement, and he had no trouble coming up with excuses. He was sure Elijah would disappear again (verse 12), and when Ahab did not find him he would, as kings in those times were inclined to do, kill the messenger for being the bearer of bad tidings. Elijah responded to Obadiah's fears with this firm word: 'As the LORD of hosts lives, before whom I stand, I will surely present myself to him today' (verse 15). In those words, Obadiah heard the Word of God and the reluctance of his heart crumbled. Just as the Word of God overpowered the hardness of Ahab's heart and caused him to answer Elijah's summons, so it overpowered the reluctance and half-heartedness of Obadiah and propelled him into obedience.

Are not believers today a lot like Obadiah? We see the evil of our times and we know something must be done, but we want the Lord to accomplish his work without us. We want to get by with doing a few things in secret or we want to sit on the sidelines and cheer, but we do not want personal, costly involvement. We may rest assured that if we are ever to see true spiritual revival in our day it is going to occur as a result of the Word of God taking hold of the church again. We keep wanting the Lord to address the Ahabs of this world, but the first thing the Lord does in revival is address his own people. This is, in my estimation, what the Lord is doing now. While many are concerned about the evils of the nation, the Lord is looking at the ills of the church. He is calling each of his children to repudiate their half-heartedness and their private discipleship and be holy channels for his Word. May God help us to hear his call.

8

What is Causing
the Trouble?

Then it happened, when Ahab saw Elijah, that Ahab said to him, 'Is that you, O troubler of Israel?' And he answered, 'I have not troubled Israel, but you and your father's house have, in that you have foresaken the commandments of the LORD, and you have followed the Baals. Now, therefore, send and gather all Israel to me on Mount Carmel, the four hundred and fifty prophets of Baal, and the four hundred prophets of Asherah, who eat at Jezebel's table.' So Ahab sent for all the children of Israel, and gathered the prophets together on Mount Carmel. And Elijah came to all the people, and said, 'How long will you falter between two opinions? If the LORD is God, follow Him; but if Baal, then follow him.' But the people answered him not a word.

1 Kings 18:17-21

Elijah and Ahab were in agreement about one thing. There was trouble in Israel. As far as Ahab was concerned, the trouble was the three-and-a-half-year drought that had a stranglehold on the nation. Furthermore, there could be absolutely no doubt at all about who was responsible for the drought. It was Elijah who had burst into Ahab's presence and announced that there would be no rain in Israel until he, Elijah, said so (17:1). It was all very simple to Ahab—the drought was the trouble and Elijah was the cause. When he finally stood before Elijah he wasted no time in pointing the finger of blame: 'Is that you, O troubler of Israel?' (18:17).

Elijah had a completely different view of things. He knew that the drought was not Israel's trouble at all, simply a consequence of the real trouble. The real trouble was the sin Ahab and the people of Israel had embraced. Ahab thought that if the drought were removed then all would be well. Elijah knew that only if the sin were removed would the drought be ended and the nation prosper again.

This passage ought to be of great interest to each and every child of God for one very good reason—the debate of Elijah and Ahab is still going on. There is no argument today on whether our society is in trouble. Only the most obtuse conclude otherwise. Homes continue to fall apart at an astonishing pace. Sexual perversions of the rawest sort are endorsed and dignified on television, in the movies and in magazines. Drug addiction, crime, corruption in business and government, dishonesty in the workplace are all prime indicators that there is deep and undeniable trouble.

The hotly disputed question is the same as it was with Elijah and Ahab—what or who is the source of the trouble in our society? On this matter there is no shortage of answers. Some say lack of education is what keeps our society from dealing successfully with all its problems. Some say government is the cause of the trouble. And some, like Ahab, actually go so far as to accuse the godly of being the trouble makers. We are told, for instance, that many things—abortion, sexual perversions, pornography—are not really problems at all. The problem is Christians going around teaching that these are problems and making everyone feel guilty. Some do not hesitate to say our greatest problem is bigoted Christians trying to impose their views on everyone else.

As Elijah refused to accept the blame assigned him by Ahab, Christians today must learn to say boldly that those who stand for God are not society's enemies but its greatest friends. As we look closely at Elijah's response to the king, we notice that Elijah did not simply deny the accusation but went on to put the blame squarely where it belonged—on the violation of God's laws and on the vacillation of God's people.

In saying that the source of the trouble was the violation of God's laws (verse 18), Elijah was appealing to an objective standard. The people of Israel were not like the people of other nations. They were in a covenant relationship with God. God had called them to be his own special, prized possession and to show his glory to all the surrounding nations. No nation could have been more blessed than the nation of Israel. There was, however, more to the relationship than just blessings. The covenant also included certain stipulations and conditions. The blessings of the covenant hinged on the keeping of these and the other commandments. God made this abundantly clear time after time.

God also made explicitly clear what calamities would befall the people of Israel if they disobeyed God's commandments. One of these was drought: 'But it shall come to pass, if you do not obey the voice of the LORD your God, to observe carefully all His commandments and statutes . . . your heavens which are over your head shall be bronze, and the earth which is under you shall be iron. The Lord will change the rain of your land to powder and dust' (*Deut.* 28:15, 23-24). One of the conditions of the covenant was that the people were not to worship other gods. The first of the Ten Commandments deal with this very matter: 'You shall have no other gods before Me' (*Exod.* 20:3).

Elijah, then, had an airtight case against Ahab. It was Ahab who, despite knowing all these things, had led the people of Israel to violate the covenant, forfeit the blessings, and bring upon themselves this devastating drought.

Ahab could have stood and argued with Elijah until the cows came home, but it would have changed nothing. It was not a matter of Elijah trying to impose his religious views on Ahab. It was all written down in the law of Moses and had all been repeatedly confirmed in Israel's history—when they obeyed the covenant they were blessed and when they disobeyed they were cursed. Elijah and Ahab have long since passed off the stage of history, but the truth Elijah proclaimed still remains. If we want God's blessings we must obey his commandments! If we stubbornly refuse, we invite trouble. Even though our societies are not in a special covenant relationship with God as Israel was, God's character and his laws are the same. Whoever violates them brings trouble upon themselves. Scripture says: 'Righteousness exalts a nation, But sin is a reproach to any people' (*Prov.* 14:34).

Even though Ahab, as the leader of Israel, was primarily responsible for Israel's idolatry, he was not the sole cause of Israel's trouble. On Mount Carmel Elijah put his finger on the vacillation of God's people as another major factor in Israel's trouble. He asked them: 'How long will you falter between two opinions? If the LORD is God, follow Him; but if Baal, then follow him.' It is important for us to realize that the people of Israel, in embracing Baal, had not completely repudiated the worship of God—they had been attempting to create a synthesis between God and Baal. As we have already seen, even Ahab himself appears to have been a syncretist. The names he gave his children indicate that he had not rejected the worship of God. Although his wife, Jezebel, and her prophets were totalitarian in their viewpoint and were working to have Baal worshipped without rival, the king and the rest of the people had not yet gone to this extreme. They wanted the best of both worlds. They wanted what God could give them, but they also wanted what Baal could supposedly give them.

Yet the harsh truth is that, in essence, this kind of syncretism is just a form of wavering. The people of Israel had wavered for years between God and Baal, but now they were wavering even more. The fact that a prophet of God had announced a drought and it had come with stunning severity must have injected serious doubts in their minds about whether they had been wise to follow Baal. At the same time, they were reluctant to turn their backs on Baal. The worship of the same god their neighbours worshipped made them feel like they were in step with the times. In addition to that, the sexual rites which were part and parcel of Baal's worship gave them a great deal of pleasure and gratification. It would be difficult to give up that which pandered to their flesh and go back to the moral purity demanded by God. On the other hand, they had to have rain and they had to have it fast. If Baal could not deliver it and God could, giving up the sexual rites would be a small price to pay. Pulled in opposite directions, the people of Israel just wavered. At one moment they were ready to renounce Baal-worship and return to God, then the next moment they were asking how they could ever think of such a thing.

As soon as the people were gathered before him, therefore,

Elijah launched a frontal assault on this mentality. He pointed out that their position was untenable; that they had been trying to reconcile two mutually exclusive principles. The God of their fathers claimed the very same thing they had attributed to Baal—control of the weather and the fertility of the land. Both could not be right. One had to be wrong. It did not matter how enjoyable and pleasurable the worship of Baal was, if he were not the true god they would lose everything. It did not matter that God demanded holiness. If he were the true God they would gain everything.

Are you wondering what all this has to do with us? The fact is that many of God's people today are just as enamoured with syncretism as the people of Israel were in Elijah's day. They do not want to renounce the worship of the true God, but neither do they want to turn a deaf ear to the popular teachings and opinions of the day. They want to keep all their options open. If God is out there and if he is what he claims to be, they are afraid to run the risk of offending him. So they try to keep appearances up by going through the motions of religion.

On the other hand, they want to feel like they are in step with the times. They do not want to be a laughing-stock at work or at school. If everyone there agrees that we all evolved; that our highest purpose is to develop a sense of self-worth; that abortion and sexual promiscuity are okay; that the worst sin is dogmatism, then it becomes very easy for the Christians to begin to subtract from their faith the more offensive teachings and to add to it the popular dogmas of the day. There is only one hitch: after our attempts to synthesize these kinds of conflicting beliefs we are left with something that is not Christianity at all.

Ultimately, there is only one question which really matters. It is not what everyone else believes or does. It is not what gives us the most pleasure and comfort. It is this—What is true? If Christianity is not true, it is time to throw away the whole thing—lock, stock and barrel—and to fling ourselves into wholehearted devotion to the popular opinions and lifestyles of the day. But if Christianity is true, it is time to stop trying to water it down and begin living it properly. The crying need of the hour is for Christians to stop thinking there is some light in the world's darkness and some darkness in God's light. Christians cannot be fence-sitters in a world that cries out for direction and guidance. Jesus himself addressed this matter of vacillation in no uncertain terms: 'No one can serve two masters; for either he will hate the one and love the other, or else he will be loyal to the one and despise the other. You cannot serve God and mammon' (*Matt.* 6:24).

The people of Israel, then, were as much at fault as their king. Perhaps they, too, wanted to blame Elijah for their troubles. It is always easy to blame others for our own flaws. It is much harder to fall on our faces before God and repent. Repentance was, however, the only thing that would save Israel then, and it is the only thing which will save us now.

9

Who Has
the Answers?

Then Elijah said to the people, 'I alone am left a prophet of the LORD; but Baal's prophets are four hundred and fifty men. Therefore let them give us two bulls; and let them choose one bull for themselves, cut it in pieces, and lay it on the wood, but put no fire under it; and I will prepare the other bull, and lay it on the wood but put no fire under it. Then you call on the name of your gods, and I will call on the name of the LORD; and the god who answers by fire, He is God.' So all the people answered and said, 'It is well spoken.' Now Elijah said to the prophets of Baal, 'Choose one of bull for yourselves and prepare it first, for you are many; and call on the name of your god, but put no fire under it.' So they took the bull which was given them, and prepared it, and called on the name of Baal from morning even till noon, saying, 'O Baal, hear us!' But there was no voice; no one answered. And they leaped about the altar which they had made. And so it was, at noon, that Elijah mocked them and said, 'Cry aloud, for he is a god; either he is meditating, or he is busy, or he is on a journey, or perhaps he is sleeping and must be awakened.' So they cried aloud, and cut themselves, as was their custom, with knives and lances, until the blood gushed out on them. And it was so, when midday was past, that they prophesied until the time of the offering of the evening sacrifice. But there was no voice; no one answered, no one paid attention.

1 Kings 18:22-29

The key word in this passage is 'answer'. It was agreed by the people, the prophets of Baal, and Elijah that the God 'who answers by fire' would be acknowledged as God in Israel (verse 24). The prophets of Baal prepared their sacrifice and began to cry out 'O Baal, hear us!' (verse 26). The sad culmination of all their efforts is recorded in these sombre words: 'But there was no voice; no one answered, no one paid attention' (verse 29).

People are looking for answers today. The age-old questions of where we came from, why we are here, and where we are going refuse to melt away. Some think the answer is not to look for any answer; they try to lose themselves in a whirl of pleasure and materialism or in some mind-altering substance that keeps them from having to face reality. For them, life is not something to be seriously contemplated. Life just happens and they try to cope with its harshness and pain by dulling their senses.

There are, however, multitudes of people who see the folly of trying to slip through life in an unthinking way. They know this life has great significance and they want to know how to live it. There are all sorts of avenues for those who want to think seriously about life, and one of those avenues is religion. Almost all religions profess to have the answers to the meaning and purpose of this life. I say 'almost' because some religious teachers seem to pride themselves on not having any answers. They decry anything that smacks of certainty. To them life is one endless quest for truth. If one ever finds truth the quest is over, and they so enjoy the quest that they do not want it to end. Most people have no trouble seeing the folly of this kind of thinking. They know that if a particular religion has no answers then there is no need to pursue it. This is the reason so many liberal churches have dwindling congregations. Most people just are not interested in a religion that has all questions and no answers. We have all got plenty of questions ourselves and we need answers.

The difficulty is not over by merely restricting ourselves to those religions which claim to have the answers for life. Religions can contradict each other. What does one do then? This was the case with the people of Israel in Elijah's time. They were faced with diametrically opposite claims. Both the God of their fathers and the god of the Canaanite nations, Baal, claimed to be in control of the weather. Which of the two was the true God? The prophets of Baal were confident their god was the right one and they did not hesitate to accept Elijah's challenge. Fire was no problem for a god who specialized in sending rain upon the earth. All that was needed was one bolt of lightning to set their sacrifice blazing. They would then seize Elijah, put him to death, and Israel would belong to Baal for all time.

It may have sounded simple when Elijah first stated the challenge, but it turned out to be an impossible one. The prophets of Baal cried to their god from morning to evening. They even resorted to leaping upon the altar and to cutting themselves with knives and lances, but all to no avail. There are three main things in this sad episode for us to learn about discerning which religion does have the answers to life's most fundamental questions.

Note first that it is possible for a religion to be popular, yet still not be true. The prophets of Baal had a distinct numerical advantage on this particular day. There were four hundred and fifty of them and another four hundred prophets of Baal's female counterpart (verse 19). In addition to those impressive numbers, Baal enjoyed the support of the king and queen and the majority of the population. Even though the people had refused to commit themselves when Elijah accused them of wavering between two opinions (verse 21), it is safe to say that Baal worship would not have flourished in Israel if the majority of the citizenship had not supported it.

All of these numbers meant nothing. Baal was still unable to provide fire for his sacrifice. Our society sorely needs to understand that just because something is popular does not make it right. The first thing some do when they begin to cast around for answers is to look at what the most or the best are following. If fifty-one percent of the people subscribe to a belief or a view they assume it must be correct. Or if a particular élite—the rich, the intelligentsia, the famous—believe certain things and act a certain way, some people tend to follow their lead slavishly. Reincarnation, for example, has been a popular belief in recent years. There is not a shred of evidence to support it, but many have uncritically accepted it because it is a popular belief of the avant-garde.

Jesus had something to say about following what is popular. He observed that there are only two roads in all of life. One is narrow and leads to eternal life. The other is broad and leads to eternal destruction. Which of these two is the popular path? Jesus said it is the broad road! His message is clear—follow what is popular and you will end up in hell! (*Matt.* 7:13-14).

A second thing we learn about finding the religion with the answer is that it is possible for a particular religion to move the emotions and still not be true. The prophets of Baal did not lack emotion in their attempts to get Baal to hear them. They would have won any emotion contest hands down. They cried and leapt and even cut themselves in their frenzy. When Elijah's turn finally came he seemed dull, drab and lifeless by comparison.

This is another much-needed word for us. How many in our day make their decision regarding the veracity of a religion on the basis of emotion? If a religion makes them feel good they assume it must be correct and true. It has always been Satan's grand design to get us to judge what is true by what appeals to us emotionally. This is exactly what he did with Eve in the Garden of Eden. He pointed out how desirable and appealing was the fruit of the forbidden tree and asked her to make her decision on that basis rather than on the basis of what God had commanded.

This is not to say that there should be no emotion at all in religion. Thank God, true religion does move us emotionally, but while true religion does move us, everything that moves us is not true religion. Just because someone says 'Hallelujah' does not mean he has the real thing.

What, then, is the distinguishing mark of true religion? How do we know which religion really has the answer? The contest on Mount Carmel clearly teaches that the true religion is the one in which there are objective demonstrations of the presence of God. The key word is 'objective'. It means something real and observable; something that can be seen and touched. Elijah called for an objective demonstration. Fire was something that could be seen, and, if one were foolish enough, touched. In calling for fire, Elijah was calling for something that everyone on Mount Carmel could see. He did not want the people to leave the mountain doubtful as to whether something had happened or not.

The prophets of Baal had plenty of opportunity to show the people that their religion was based on something real. Perhaps at the end of the long day one of these prophets said to the others: 'Even though we didn't see literal fire, I believe that Baal answered our prayer and sent fire in our hearts.' That explanation may have satisfied them for a while, but the satisfaction could not last long. Because when Elijah prayed fire fell! And it was not just a fire that he could feel in his heart. It was such a consuming fire that it licked up the water Elijah had poured on the sacrifice as well as the dust around the altar. When that fire fell, it was powerful, vivid and indisputable.

Which religion really has the answer for perplexed men and women who are seeking the meaning of life? It is not the religion that is temporarily popular. It is not the religion which titillates the senses. It is the religion which is based on objective truth—Christianity! Take a tour through the Bible and you will see God constantly breaking into human affairs and powerfully demonstrating that he is present in this universe and that we must some day give account of ourselves to him. He demonstrated his presence and his reality in the flood of Noah's time, in the plagues on Pharaoh and the Egyptians, when the walls of Jericho came crashing down, and so on.

But the greatest single objective demonstration of God's reality is Jesus Christ. His life was an unbroken display of the power and presence of God. He opened blind eyes and deaf ears. He caused the lame to walk again. He raised three people from the dead. As a final and unanswerable proof of God's power and presence in his life, Jesus Christ arose from death and he lives today. The resurrection is not just a matter of some people saying they feel that Jesus is alive in their hearts. He really lives. Angels appeared and talked with those who came to the tomb. The tomb itself was empty. Hundreds of people saw the risen Christ. This is an objective reality!

Are you looking for answers to the meaning of your life? There is no need to look any further. Jesus Christ is the answer. He is 'the way, the truth, and the life' (*John* 14:6). Bow before him in repentance of your sins and believe in what he has done for your salvation, and you can stop searching for the truth and start rejoicing that you have found it!

10

Steps to Revival

Then Elijah said to all the people, 'Come near to me.' So all the people came near to him. And he repaired the altar of the LORD that was broken down. And Elijah took twelve stones, according to the number of the tribes of the sons of Jacob, to whom the word of the LORD had come, saying, 'Israel shall be your name.' Then with the stones he built an altar in the name of the LORD; and he made a trench around the altar large enough to hold two seahs of seed. And he put the wood in order, cut the bull in pieces, and laid it on the wood, and said, 'Fill four waterpots with water, and pour it on the burnt sacrifice and on the wood.' Then he said, 'Do it a second time,' and they did it a second time; and he said, 'Do it a third time,' and they did it a third time. So water ran all around the altar; and he even filled the trench with water. And it came to pass, at the time of the offering of the evening sacrifice, that Elijah the prophet came near and said, 'LORD God of Abraham, Isaac, and Israel, let it be known this day that You are God in Israel, and that I am Your servant, and that I have done all these things at Your word. Hear me, O LORD, hear me, that this people may know that You are the LORD God, and that You have turned their hearts back to You again.' Then the fire of the LORD fell and consumed the burnt sacrifice, and the wood and the stones and the dust, and it licked up the water that was in the trench. Now when all the people saw it, they fell on theur faces; and said, 'The LORD, He is God! The LORD, He is God!' And Elijah said to them, 'Seize the prophets of Baal! Do not let one of them escape!' So they seized them; and Elijah brought them down to the Brook Kishon and executed them there.

1 Kings 18:30–40

It is indisputable that something astonishing and profound took place on Mount Carmel. The day began with the people of Israel in a non-committal mood. Elijah had framed the issue in clear and sensible terms: 'If the LORD is God, follow Him; but if Baal, then follow him.' To this logical proposition 'the people said nothing' (verse 21). How different things were at the end of the day! Instead of refusing to decide between God and Baal, the people were now falling on their faces and crying: 'The LORD, He is God! The LORD, He is God!' (verse 39).

This transformation was so remarkable that many people have not hesitated to call it a revival or a spiritual awakening, but that is probably going too far. True revival leaves a lasting mark on society, but the experience on Mount Carmel seems to have affected the people in a very temporary way. After the fire fell from heaven, Elijah went into such a deep depression that he wanted to resign from the struggle, and the people seem to have just melted away. Elijah did, of course, return to the struggle, but he never saw the end of Baal worship in his lifetime. These hard facts indicate that what happened on Mount Carmel was something less than true spiritual renewal. It is safe to assume individual Israelites were truly renewed in their faith, but the nation as a whole remained in the grip of idolatry. Even though we cannot call the Mount Carmel experience a revival, therefore, we can certainly view it as God calling the people to revival. It is a picture or a pattern for true revival, even though the people were only temporarily moved by it. What, then, does God do when he calls us to revival?

1. *He Demonstrates the Failure of Our Idols (verses 25-29).*
It was against the background of this failure of Baal that God sent fire from heaven and was acknowledged as the true God. One of the things which ought to give us hope at the moment

is that so many of the things we have previously trusted in have utterly failed: things such as science, materialism, education, government. Perhaps another failure or two will bring us to the point where we are ready to turn to God.

2. *He Exposes Our Sin and Calls Us to Repentance*
   (verses 30-32).

This is pictured by the altar Elijah repaired. To understand the significance of Elijah's action we must keep in mind the significance of the altar in God's covenant with Israel. There the sacrifice was made for sin, and only on the basis of sacrifice could God have communion with people.

There were in the land of Israel several altars to the Lord before the temple in Jerusalem was built. These altars, however, were not to be used after the temple came into existence. So why did Elijah make use of this altar on Mount Carmel? The reason is because this was an unusual time in the history of the Lord's people. Two tribes made up the kingdom of Judah and ten tribes made up the kingdom of Israel. The temple was in Judah, but Elijah was dealing with the people of Israel, people who had been shut off from going to the temple in Jerusalem. In order for these people to worship the Lord, it was necessary for them to use the old altars which had been used before the temple was built.

The fact that this altar was broken down shows how low the worship of God had sunk in the days of Elijah. In all probability, Jezebel and her prophets were responsible for the destruction of the altar (19:10), but faith in Israel had reached such a state that no one had either the interest or the courage to restore it. It is interesting that this altar had been broken down at a time when Ahab was striving for a synthesis between the worship of Baal and the worship of God. We have already explored how impossible it is to synthesize successfully the false and the true. Try to synthesize the truth of God with falsehood and the truth will always suffer. M.B. Van't Veer has pointed out that: 'Whenever the church and the world mingle, it is not the church that sets its stamp on the world but the world that sets it stamp on the church until only the world is left.'[4]

It is significant that Elijah used twelve stones to repair the altar, one for each of the original twelve tribes of Israel. In so doing he was reminding the people of the clearly defined will of God for their lives, and exposing their failure to comply with that will. One sin had led to another in Israel. Because of the sinfulness of King Solomon the kingdom was divided. Because of the sinfulness of Jeroboam idol worship had been introduced into the ten tribes. Because of the sinfulness of Ahab the worship of Baal had flourished. The people themselves were not guiltless in all of this ungodliness, for they had tolerated and participated in it. In rebuilding this altar, Elijah was taking the people back to what God demanded—one kingdom completely devoted to his service and governed by his laws. This may all seem very remote and irrelevant to us, but the truth is that no great work of revival begins until people are powerfully reminded of the clearly defined will of God in Scripture and are shown how seriously they have departed from that will.

3. *He Forces Us to Look Solely to Him (v. 32-35).*
This is pictured by the water Elijah poured on and around the sacrifice. This part of the story always causes some to wonder where Elijah got this amount of water after three and a half years of drought. Perhaps there was a deep well on Mount Carmel that had not yet run dry. It seems more likely that Elijah pre-arranged for the water to be brought up from the

4   Van't Veer, p. 245.

Mediterranean Sea, which was at the foot of the mountain.

In pouring this water on the sacrifice Elijah again called the attention of the people of Israel to the number twelve, serving as another reminder of God's will for the nation. But Elijah's principal purpose in pouring water over the sacrifice was to eliminate all other explanations for the sacrifice's being consumed. He did not want anyone to suggest that he had somehow sneaked a burning coal under the sacrifice or used any other kind of trickery. When they saw the water being poured on the altar until it stood in the trench Elijah had dug around it the people would realize that it was humanly impossible for the sacrifice to burn.

The lesson we urgently need to draw from Elijah's action is that revival cannot be produced by human ingenuity and cleverness. Perhaps the primary reason we have not yet seen a great spiritual awakening this century is that we have not yet reached the water-pouring stage. We have not shut ourselves up unto God as our only hope. As long as we think we can produce revival with our clever programmes and promotions we may rest assured that we will never see one. Only when the church reaches the point of desperation—in which she pours water on her own abilities and casts herself wholly upon the Lord—will she ever see true revival.

Elijah's pouring of the water also teaches us to have hope in the midst of what appears to be an impossible situation. How could a soaked sacrifice ever burn? Yet what is impossible to us is not impossible to God! He is the one who taught Ezekiel that even the driest of bones can be incorporated into living bodies again if he, the Lord, says the word! (*Ezek.* 37:1-14). How many times has the church seemed to be facing an impossible task? How many times has it seemed that wickedness was just too great and the cause of God was ready to perish from the face of the earth? Elijah's water pouring urges us never to despair. It is always too early to give up on God.

4.   *He Sets Us to Prayer (verses 36-38).*
This, of course, is pictured in the prayer Elijah prayed. Several features of this prayer call for attention.

   i.   *The timing of Elijah's prayer.*
Twice we are told in this chapter that Elijah's prayer was offered at the time of the evening sacrifice (verses 29, 36), i.e. the same time the sacrifice was offered in the temple in Jerusalem. It is clear Elijah deliberately timed his sacrifice to coincide with that sacrifice as an additional reminder to the people of what God's will was for the nation and how far they had strayed from it.

   ii.   *The basis of Elijah's prayer.*
In constructing his challenge to the prophets of Baal, Elijah did not just pick the idea of fire from heaven out of the air. His challenge was squarely based on God's Word. The Lord had on previous occasions sent fire from heaven to consume a sacrifice. The first time it occurred was when the whole priestly system was instituted. God testified to his own truthfulness and to the legitimacy of his office-bearers by setting the sacrifice on fire (*Lev.* 9:24). It happened again with Gideon (*Judg.* 6:17) and with King David (*1 Chron.* 21:26). In each of these cases the issues were essentially the same as they were in Elijah's day. There was in each instance a need for God to bear witness to his reality and presence.

   The vast majority of Christians seem to think praying in faith means simply convincing ourselves that whatever we want will come to pass. In truth, the prayer of faith is praying on the basis of what God has revealed in his Word. We may rest assured the prophets of Baal had what most people consider to be 'faith', but they received no answer because the power is not in the faith but in the only true and living God.

iii. *The motivation of Elijah's prayer (verses 36-37).*

It was first and foremost a prayer for God to glorify himself by confirming to the people that he was indeed God. How much of our praying is for the glory of God? Could it be we are not seeing revival because our motivation is all wrong? It is possible for us to seek revival simply out of the desire for our lives to be free from the misery and woe generated by an ungodly society. If that is our motivation, we shall seek in vain. If, on the other hand, we pray for revival because we are tired of seeing God's name ridiculed and his laws spat upon and want to see him vindicated and honoured, we have every reason to be confident he will hear and answer.

iv. *The tone of the prayer (verse 37).*

It was not offered by Elijah in a casual, take-it-or-leave-it manner, but was fervent and intense. Elijah pleaded with God: 'Hear me, O LORD, Hear me'. Revival praying is always fervent praying. Revival praying despises empty slogans and tired phrases. It declares war on simply going through the motions and earnestly wrestles with God.

The easiest thing in the world is to say that we want revival. But it is quite another matter to seek it earnestly. If we want to know how serious we are about revival, all we have to do is compare ourselves with what Elijah did on Mount Carmel. Can we truly say we are willing to face our sins and deal with them? Can we say we are ready to cast ourselves solely on God? Can we say we are ready to pray as Elijah did? If we can say these things, we may yet see fire from heaven in this day of monstrous ungodliness.

11

The Fire of Judgement and the Flood of Blessing

Then the fire of the LORD fell and consumed the burnt sacrifice, and the wood and the stones and the dust, and it licked up the water that was in the trench. Now when all the people saw it, they fell on theur faces; and said, 'The LORD, He is God! The LORD, He is God!' And Elijah said to them, 'Seize the prophets of Baal! Do not let one of them escape!' So they seized them; and Elijah brought them down to the Brook Kishon and executed them there. Then Elijah said to Ahab, 'Go up, eat and drink; for there is the sound of abundance of rain.' So Ahab went up to eat and drink. And Elijah went up to the top of Carmel; then he bowed down on the ground, and put his face between his knees. and said to his servant, 'Go up now, look toward the sea.' So he went up and looked, and said, 'There is nothing.' And seven times he said, 'Go again.' Then it came to pass the seventh time, that he said, 'There is a cloud, as small as a man's hand, rising out of the sea!' So he said, 'Go up, say to Ahab, "Prepare your chariot, and go down before the rain stops you."' Now it happened in the meantime that the sky became black with clouds and wind, and there was a heavy rain. So Ahab rode away and went to Jezreel. Then the hand of the LORD came upon Elijah; and he girded up his loins and ran ahead of Ahab to the entrance of Jezreel.

1 Kings 18:38–46

As the people of Israel gathered on Mount Carmel to witness the showdown between Elijah and the prophets of Baal they thought their great need was rain. When Elijah suggested fire as the means to determine the true and living God the people may very well have scratched their heads in wonderment. Why not make rain the determining factor? The last thing anybody in Israel wanted to hear about or see was fire. For three-and-a-half years the drought had made the whole nation seem continually ablaze.

Elijah was also concerned about rain, but, having been deeply schooled in the truths of God, he knew that if the people of Israel saw the fire of God the rain would come. Both the fire and the rain are full of instruction and spiritual significance for us, and we must, therefore, give attention to them.

1. *The Fire of God's Judgement (verses 38-40).*
Elijah was not interested in fire alone, but fire that consumed a sacrifice. Why did he insist on this? If he wanted fire from heaven to be the proof of the true God, why not simply select a bush for the fire to burn?

The whole sacrificial system was built on the premise that man stands guilty before a holy God, that he has broken God's commandments and cannot have fellowship or communion with God until something is done about his sin. In making a sacrifice, the sinner was symbolically owning his guilt and transferring it to the animal. He was acknowledging he was worthy of death himself but was offering the death of the animal as his own death. In other words, the basic idea behind the sacrifice was substitution. The animal became the substitute for the sinner.

Elijah knew the people of Israel stood guilty before God, that they richly deserved to die for their sins, and that God could have consumed them with fire from heaven and been fully justified in doing so. In asking God to consume the sacrifice, Elijah was asking him to accept the animal as a substitute for the people. When the people saw the fire from heaven they immediately cried out: 'The LORD, He is God! The LORD, He is God!' In other words, they accepted and owned the sacrifice as their own. Although they did not realize it, the experience of Elijah and the people of Israel that day pictured and foreshadowed the death of the Lord Jesus Christ on the cross. The Lord Jesus went to that cross as a sacrifice for sinners. He received the penalty of God's broken law so we might be spared. The cross is nothing less than God's holy wrath bypassing sinners and striking Jesus!

It is significant that nothing is said about the reaction of the prophets of Baal to the fire which consumed Elijah's sacrifice. We are plainly told the people acknowledged God, but what about these false prophets? The account we have is silent on this, but I think that we can safely assume they hardened their hearts against the truth of God and refused to join the people in saying: 'The LORD, He is God!' We can be confident about this because the very next thing we read is that Elijah immediately ordered the prophets to be executed.

At this point, we have to consider whether Elijah was right to demand their execution. Many do not hesitate to denounce this as a cruel, barbaric act. They completely ignore several facts. First, the law of God clearly required that any prophet who led the people of Israel to worship false gods be put to death (*Deut.* 13:1-5). Second, these false prophets were murderers themselves in two distinct ways. There is every reason to believe they actively participated in the systematic elimination of the true prophets of God (*1 Kings* 19:10). On top of that, they were guilty of indirectly causing great loss of life by fostering the sin that brought the drought upon the nation.

Instead of denouncing the execution of these false prophets, we should take to heart the great lesson which is taught here. The prophets of Baal refused to acknowledge the fire of God in consuming the sacrifice and so they experienced the fire of his judgement. Some say they are glad we are serving the New Testament God of love instead of the Old Testament God of wrath, but the Bible makes it clear that there is only one God and he never changes. Elijah's God speaks through the pages of the New Testament to say all who do not acknowledge and own the fire that consumed Jesus' sacrifice on the cross will experience the fire of his eternal judgement!

In insisting that the test for the true God be fire consuming a sacrifice, therefore, Elijah was not ignoring the need for rain but was going to the very heart of the problem. He was linking the blessing the people desired (rain), with something being done about their sin (the sacrifice). The truth is the drought that had broiled the nation was never the primary problem, but was the result of it. The drought would never have happened if the nation had not turned from the commandments of God to embrace the worship of Baal. Only when that sin was dealt with was the way cleared for God to bless Israel.

2. *The Flood of God's Blessing (verses 41-46).*
Immediately after giving the command to execute the false prophets Elijah begins to pray for rain. Yet a question which leaps instantly to mind is—if the sacrifice for sin removed the obstacle between God and the people, why did the rain not immediately begin to fall? This is so typical of us. We want God's blessings to fall automatically upon us without any effort on our part. Elijah teaches us that God has appointed certain channels through which those blessings flow; the sacrifice removed the obstacle and opened the channel, but the channel still had to be used. Here we find Elijah making use of that

open channel on behalf of the people of Israel. In so doing he teaches us how to use this channel. In other words, he teaches us how to pray.

The nature of effective praying is a common theme in the life of Elijah, and we see those same ingredients again here:

i. *Elijah's great confidence in God.*

He was so certain of the outcome he even told Ahab to begin eating and drinking in celebration. Rain was definitely on the way (verse 41). He had such bold confidence because he trusted in God's historical promises that drought would come if the people turned to false gods and rain would come if they turned back to the true God (*Deut.* 11:13-17), and in the present word to him from God that the rain would appear (18:1). The fact that Elijah had a promise, however, did not keep him from praying. God does not make promises so we will not pray, but so that we will be moved to pray with assurance. The promises give us firm ground on which to place our prayers.

ii. *The intensity of Elijah's praying.*

Elijah 'bowed down on the ground, and put his face between his knees' (verse 42). He was not content merely to mouth empty slogans but poured his heart and soul into his praying.

iii. *The persistence of Elijah's praying.*

Seven times Elijah prayed for the blessing of rain, and only after the seventh time did his servant see a small cloud in the shape of a man's hand. A. W. Pink summarizes it neatly: 'a man's hand had been raised in supplication and had, as it were, left its shadow on the heavens.' [5]

If we learn nothing else from Elijah's life except how to pray, we will have learned volumes. Our praying tends to be self-ishly motivated. We pray for things God has never promised

5 Arthur W. Pink, *The Life of Elijah*, The Banner of Truth, Edinburgh, 1991, p. 188.

and expect him to grant them. We pray casually instead of fervently and intensely. And we regard persistence in prayer as an indication of lack of faith. To us faith means asking God one time for something and to ask again is tantamount to admitting we do not expect to receive it. How Elijah's prayer rebukes this kind of praying!

After his servant spied the cloud, Elijah knew a cloudburst was upon them so he urged Ahab to prepare immediately to get his chariot off the mountain (verse 44). As Ahab rode away to Jezreel, Elijah ran before him. This seems to many to be just another fantastic element that makes the whole story of Elijah unbelievable, since Jezreel was about sixteen miles from Mount Carmel. How could a man possibly out-distance a chariot over such a long way? The writer of 1 Kings explains this feat by simply saying, 'the hand of the Lord came upon Elijah' (verse 46). If God is, by definition, all-powerful, why should we stumble at his giving Elijah enough power to do this?

We must not get so immersed in the details of the feat itself that we lose sight of the lesson it was designed to teach. Elijah had that day, by the grace of God, restored the communion between Israel and the people of the Lord, a communion which resulted in the blessings of the covenant being restored. By running before Ahab's chariot he was delivering to the king a powerful object lesson. Elijah was the bearer of the Word of God, and his running showed Ahab exactly what he, as the theocratic king, must do to keep that channel of communion open. He had to follow the Word of God! By running all the way to Jezreel, Elijah demonstrated that the Word of God must not only be followed but that it was sufficient. No demands can be placed upon it that it cannot bear.

At first glance, the fire and the rain on Mount Carmel may seem like odd occurrences in a bizarre narrative, but in reality they convey timeless spiritual truths. The fire tells us there can be no communion with God until sin is dealt with. The rain tells us that communion with God and the blessings of God always come through the channels of prayer and obedience to the Word of God. We are wise if we come away from Mount Carmel with a renewed understanding of these vital truths.

12

The Stress
of the Struggle

And Ahab told Jezebel all that Elijah had done, also how he had executed all the prophets with the sword. Then Jezebel sent a messenger to Elijah, saying, 'So let the gods do to me, and more also, if I do not make your life as the life of one of them by tomorrow about this time.' And when he saw that, he arose and ran for his life, and went to Beersheba, which belongs to Judah, and left his servant there. But he himself went a day's journey into the wilderness, and came and sat under a broom tree And he prayed that he might die, and said, 'It is enough! Now, LORD,' take my life, for I am no better than my fathers!' Then as he lay and slept under a broom tree, suddenly an angel touched him, and said to him, 'Arise and eat.' Then he looked, and there by his head was a cake baked on coals, and a jar of water. So he ate and drank, and lay down again. And the angel of the LORD came back the second time, and touched him, and said, 'Arise and eat, because the journey is too great for you.' So he arose, and ate and drank; and he went in the strength of that food forty days and forty nights as far as Horeb, the mountain of God.

1 Kings 19:1-8

Never has there been a more abrupt and dramatic change in a man than the one that occurred in Elijah immediately after the events on Mount Carmel. One moment he was running triumphantly before Ahab; the next he was running frantically from Jezebel. The man who had boldly faced four hundred and fifty hostile prophets now trembles at the threat of one woman. The man who had prayed until the life-giving rain came now prays for his own life to be ended. The man who walked with a sure and certain step on the mountain top of victory now wallows in the valley of despair.

The very fact the Bible relates such a remarkable turnabout in the life of Elijah tells us something about the nature of this book. Any mere human author would never allow the character of such a great hero to be tarnished and besmirched by such a humiliating nose-dive. But the Bible has God for its author and our profit for its purpose, so Elijah's weaknesses are not tastefully swept aside but are laid bare before our eyes. How can we profit from Elijah's sad experience? We must focus on both the stress that triggered his despair and the grace which finally triumphed over it.

It is impossible for us to know exactly what was running through Elijah's mind as he ran ahead of Ahab's chariot. He had been locked in a life and death struggle with the forces of evil, and those forces had now been decisively and brilliantly defeated. It is unlikely Elijah thought his victory would cause Jezebel to have a change of heart and to acknowledge that Baal was an empty vanity. However, he may have allowed himself to nurture the hope that Ahab would be emboldened to put Jezebel in her place and not allow her to impose her false religion upon his kingdom.

Whatever hopes Elijah nurtured, they were soon dashed to the ground. Upon their arrival in Jezreel, Ahab went in to tell

Jezebel of the developments while Elijah waited outside. Jezebel was in no mood to concede anything but flew into a rage and vowed that she would do to Elijah what he had done to her prophets. Why she did not send someone at that moment to kill Elijah can only be explained in terms of the restraining grace of the Lord.

As soon as word of her threat reached Elijah, he fled. He left his servant at Beersheba, went a day's journey into the wilderness, sat down under a broom tree, and prayed to die. He did not want Jezebel to kill him, but he would have gladly accepted death from the Lord. How are we to explain such rash behaviour on Elijah's part? Could the Lord, who had preserved and protected him up to this point, not have preserved him in this situation? Why did Elijah take such extreme action in the face of one threat? It is obvious Elijah was tired of the struggle and wanted it to be over, but his problem went far deeper than that. As far as he was concerned, the outcome of the struggle was itself in doubt. S.G. DeGraaf explains Elijah's outlook in these terms: 'He saw the Lord contending as a human being does, with uncertain prospects for victory.' [6]

Elijah may very well have reasoned something like this: 'If a fireball from heaven and a heavy rain doesn't make Jezebel see the light, nothing can.' His basic problem, then, was that he wanted Mount Carmel to bring an end to the struggle, and it did not. Although it was an astounding display of God's glory and power, it failed to usher in Utopia.

It is possible for Elijah's despair to grip us. If we are not careful we can get a false impression about the nature of the Christian's walk in this world. We see iniquity swirling all around us, and we begin to talk about the need for revival and to pray urgently for revival. All of that is good, but if we are

---

6   S.G. DeGraaf, *Promise and Deliverance, Volume II*, Presbyterian and Reformed Publishing Co., St. Catherine's, Ontario, 1978, p. 260.

not careful we can fall into the trap of thinking a revival will solve all of our problems. A revival has a profound effect upon society and great improvements are made, but it does not make society perfect with one fell swoop. Evil still remains and one of the things a revival always does is stir up the forces of evil so that they unleash more hostility against the church than ever before.

Christians, like Elijah, sometimes get so tired of the struggle against evil that we will do almost anything to see an end to it. We are told to 'stop trying and start trusting', or to 'cross over into Canaan', or to seek the baptism of the Spirit, or to get filled with the Spirit, and the struggle will be over and we can pass through this life without feeling so much as a single care or without having to lift a single burden. The harsh reality Christians must face is that we will never get beyond struggling with the forces of Satan in this life. Even if a great revival breaks out, the struggle will not go away but may even be intensified.

What a sad thing it would be if the story of Elijah ended this way. Thank God for the grace of God which triumphed over Elijah's stress and despair. The Lord had not commanded Elijah to go into the wilderness. Prior to this the Bible makes it clear that every move Elijah made was in response to the leadership of the Lord, but nothing is said here about Elijah even consulting the Lord. Instead he just turned tail and ran. Even though the Lord did not send him to the wilderness, the Lord found him there. How we should rejoice that the Lord doesn't give up on us when we fail him!

Not only did the Lord find Elijah in the wilderness, he also used the wilderness to help him:

1. *God Fed Elijah.*

He sent an angel to bake him a cake and to provide him with

water. We must not miss the significance of this. Three times the Lord miraculously provided food for Elijah. The first time was at the Brook Cherith where the ravens fed him. The second time was at the widow's house in Zarephath, where he was fed by a barrel that kept replenishing itself. But here in the wilderness an angel feeds him. We are faced with an intriguing question: Why did God not use an angel to feed Elijah before, or conversely, why did God not use the ravens to feed him on all three occasions?

The answer is that each of these feedings was designed to meet Elijah's need at that particular time. The ravens bringing food they would normally have eaten themselves showed Elijah that God is indeed Lord of nature. This was the issue in his struggle with Baal, and the Lord used the ravens to confirm and strengthen Elijah's faith. The barrel at the widow's house showed Elijah that God uses his Word even when it appears that nothing is happening.

Now, by sending an angel at this particular time, the Lord did two things. Firstly, he gave Elijah much-needed reassurance. The angel was living proof that God is indeed the Lord Almighty, that he has battalions of angels at his disposal to work his will, and the outcome of the struggle, therefore, was not in doubt. (This calls to mind a later incident in the life of Elijah's successor, Elisha. His servant feared for the cause of the Lord, so Elisha asked the Lord to open the young man's eyes. As a result he saw a multitude of horses and chariots of fire surrounding him (*2 Kings* 6:15-17).) Secondly, the appearance of the angel was the Lord's way of rebuking Elijah. The angels stand constantly in God's presence watching for his signal or listening for his Word. What he commands they do quickly and gladly. Elijah, on the other hand, had fled from the field of battle without the permission of his Commander.

2. *God Reminded Elijah of His Past Faithfulness and Mercy.*
God also used the wilderness in another way. He knew Elijah intended to go to Mount Horeb. God had not commanded him to do this, but this was what Elijah planned to do. Elijah chose to go to Mount Horeb (also known as Mount Sinai) because it was there that God had established his covenant with the people of Israel. In Elijah's mind, the battle was lost and the place where it all began was the logical place to report that it had all come to an end. When Moses stood on Mount Sinai a whole nation below was eager to enter into a covenant and to serve the Lord. Now Elijah comes back to this very same mountain to say the whole enterprise has failed. As far as he was concerned, he was the only one left.

Instead of rebuking him for this desire to go to Mount Horeb, God graciously used it. He saw to it that Elijah's journey took him exactly forty days and forty nights, which was considerably longer than it should have taken. We do not know how the Lord slowed Elijah progress—he may have used dust storms or sickness or blazing heat—but we do have a better idea of why God wanted Elijah to take this long.

The Lord wanted Elijah to connect his own situation with the experience of his forefathers. They had wandered in that same wilderness for a period of forty years. As Elijah counted the days and walked past their graves in the wilderness, he would be forced to reflect deeply on the fact that the cause of God also looked lost at that time. The people had come right up to the point of conquering the land of Canaan—but then had fearfully backed away. Yet the God of grace, who had established a covenant with the people of Israel, demonstrated his faithfulness to that covenant and finally brought them into the land he had promised them. It took forty years, but God did not fail!

3.   *God Prepared Elijah for the Stillness.*

The final answer to Elijah's discouragement did not come until he finally arrived at Mount Horeb, but his experiences in the wilderness prepared his mind and heart for that answer. The grace of God was there with Elijah both in the wilderness and on the mountain. It was there to reassure, to rebuke and finally to replace the stress of the struggle with stillness.

We, like Elijah, are called to be faithful to God in the midst of a great struggle. Heaven and hell are still locked in mortal combat. Sometimes it seems that evil is winning. Truth seems forever on the scaffold and evil forever on the throne. Thank God, things are not always as they seem. God is still the Lord Almighty and his grace is sufficient for us.

13

The Stillness in
the Struggle

*And there he went into a cave, and spent the night in that place; and
behold, the word of the LORD came to him, and He said to him, 'What
are you doing here, Elijah?' So he said, 'I have been very zealous for the
LORD God of hosts: for the children of Israel have forsaken Your covenant, torn down Your altars, and killed Your prophets with the sword. I
alone am left; and they seek to take my life.' Then He said, 'Go out, and
stand on the mountain before the LORD .' And behold, the LORD passed
by, and a great and strong wind tore into the mountains and broke the
rocks in pieces before the LORD, but the LORD was not in the wind; and
after the wind an earthquake, but the LORD was not in the earthquake;
and after the earthquake a fire, but the LORD was not in the fire; and
after the fire a still small voice. So it was, when Elijah heard it, that he
wrapped his face in a mantle and went out and stood in the entrance of the
cave. And suddenly a voice came to him, and said, 'What are you doing
here, Elijah?' So he said, 'I have been very zealous for the LORD God of
hosts; because the children of Israel have forsaken Your covenant, torn down
Your altars, and killed Your prophets with the sword. I alone am left; and
they seek to take my life.' Then the LORD said to him, 'Go, return on
your way to the Wilderness of Damascus; and when you arrive, anoint
Hazael as king over Syria. Also, you shall anoint Jehu the son of Nimshi
as king over Israel. And Elisha the son of Shaphat of Abel Meholah you
shall anoint as prophet in your place. It shall be that whoever escapes the
sword of Hazael, Jehu will kill; and whoever escapes from the sword of
Jehu, Elisha will kill. Yet I have reserved seven thousand in Israel, all
whose knees have not bowed to Baal, and every mouth that has not kissed
him.'*

1 Kings 19:9-18

'It is enough' (verse 4). That is what Elijah said when he fled from Jezebel. The struggle to turn Israel back to God had become too much for him. The strain of the conflict had become so great that Elijah just wanted it to be over. Have you ever felt this way? Has the struggle to live for the Lord become too much for you? Do you find yourself longing to be just one of the crowd? Do you grow weary of always being at tension with the world, always being the 'odd man out'? Are you tired of working for the Lord and seeing precious few results?

If you find yourself feeling the strain of the struggle, this passage of Scripture is for you. Here the Lord renews Elijah's strength, not by granting his request and removing him from the struggle (for only God can decide when we 'have had enough'), but by granting him peace or stillness in the midst of the struggle.

God created this stillness in Elijah by first giving him some signs (verse 11), and then by giving him the explanation of the signs (verses 15-18). The signs and the explanation form one answer to Elijah's dilemma. The signs consisted of three very turbulent and violent forces followed by 'a still, small voice' or, as the New American Standard Bible puts it, 'a sound of a gentle blowing' (verse 11).

Before giving the signs, God asked why Elijah had deserted his post and come to the mountain. Elijah responded by saying: 'I have been very zealous for the LORD God of hosts: for the children of Israel have forsaken Your covenant, torn down Your altars, and killed Your prophets with the sword. I alone am left; and they seek to take my life.' (verse 10). After the signs, God asked again why Elijah had come to the mountain, and he gave the very same answer. It is obvious that Elijah did not understand the message the signs conveyed. God, therefore, gave Elijah the explanation of the signs. In other words, the signs were not sufficient in and of themselves. Elijah had to have the Word of God to explain and clarify them. There is a great lesson here for us. We live in a day when Christians have a great hankering for emotional and miraculous experiences. The key to finding stillness in the struggle, however, lies not in feeling emotionally moved, but in comprehending the truths of God's Word. What are the truths God taught Elijah, which cause the strain of the struggle to melt away and God's precious stillness to flow in?

1. *God is Adequate for the Struggle.*

Think again about Elijah's explanation for coming to the mountain. It is no coincidence that he referred to God as 'the LORD God of hosts'. As far as he was concerned, this was the whole issue. He had staked everything on God's being surrounded by multitudes of angels who were ready to do his bidding, on God's having the forces of nature at his disposal and subject to his authority. But now that belief did not seem to be borne out by the facts. If God were indeed God where were his hosts?

The people who had triumphantly shouted 'The LORD, He is God' on Mount Carmel had melted away leaving Elijah to face Jezebel. The fireball that fell from heaven on Mount Carmel was glorious, but where was it when Jezebel issued her threat? Yes, one angel had shown up, but only one, and he appeared well after Jezebel had made her threat. Where were the Lord's hosts when Elijah most needed them? As far as Elijah could tell, the Lord of hosts was now the Lord of one, and that one was ready to abandon ship!

After Elijah freely confessed his doubt, the Lord told him to stand on the mountain. Immediately, 'a great and strong wind tore into the mountains and broke the rocks in pieces' (verse 11). After the wind there was an earthquake, and after that there was a fire. Because the Bible tells us God was not 'in' any of these natural forces, we tend to assume they were somehow opposed to God, and we drive a wedge between them and the 'still, small voice'. The truth is, however, that even though God was not 'in' these forces, they were produced by him as he 'passed by'. They were, therefore, instruments in his hand to serve his purposes.

By using these natural forces, God caused Elijah to see that he had not been wrong in his faith, that the Lord was not without his hosts and still had all kinds of instruments at his disposal. This was made explicitly clear when the Lord told Elijah to anoint Hazael, Jehu and Elisha. The Lord was not giving up the struggle at all but was about to deploy some devastating instruments. We should take great consolation from the truth that God never lacks for instruments. His hosts are intact. He is adequate for the struggle! One of the instruments God had chosen succeeded in eliminating Baal worship from Israel (*2 Kings* 10:28).

2. *God Himself is Above the Struggle.*

After the natural forces were spent, there was 'a still, small voice'. The natural forces were God's instruments in the struggle, but he himself was in the stillness. While he is able to use turbulence to achieve his will, God himself never experiences turbulence. How sorely we need this truth! We are inclined to think of God in human terms. We see all the formidable forces of evil arrayed against his cause and we suddenly begin to think of God struggling along with uncertain prospects for victory. We begin to talk of God 'trying' to do this and 'wanting' to do that.

How different is the presentation of God in the Bible! Psalm 2, for instance, pictures the greatest of men gathering together and conspiring against God. Resenting his rule over them, they decide to revolt. What is God's response? Does he fly into a panic and hastily summon an emergency meeting of the heavenly cabinet? Not at all. The psalmist simply says: 'He who sits in the heavens shall laugh; the Lord shall hold them in derision' (*Ps.* 2:4).

Elijah was in a hand-wringing mood when he came to the mountain, but God was not wringing his hands. What Elijah did not know was that the Lord had already reserved for himself seven thousand who had not bowed the knee to Baal (verse 18). We can find plenty to wring our hands over as well. Iniquity abounds everywhere. Every vice and perversion known to man flourishes in our society. In addition to all of that, the work of the Lord inches along at a snail's pace. Sometimes it appears that the cause of God is lost and we find ourselves crying with Elijah: 'It is enough!'

But things are not always as they appear. God has his plans and he knows they will be fulfilled. He is bringing all things to the end he has appointed—that point at which God is acknowledged as all in all. The raging tides of secularism and materialism cannot thwart his purpose. The apathy and lethargy of his own people cannot thwart it. Where there is faithfulness to God, his mercy and grace will be glorified, and where there is unfaithfulness, his justice will be glorified; but, mark it down, God will be glorified!

3. *We are Called to Obey God in the Midst of the Struggle.*
When we learn the first two truths of stillness—God is adequate for the struggle and God is above the struggle—we are tempted to think there is absolutely nothing for us to do. Immorality abounds? Leave God to take care of it! Families disintegrate? God will work it out! Churches falter? Let God handle it! If God is above the struggle, we should, according to some, be above the struggle. To think this way is to miscon-

strue the teaching of Scripture. God is above the struggle because he is the sovereign ruler of this universe, and sin cannot ultimately diminish or defeat his sovereignty. But it is this same sovereign God who has decreed that we be his instruments in the struggle. God's message to Elijah was not: 'I have got everything under control, so you just go back, sit in your cave, and enjoy life.' God's message was: 'I have got everything under control, so you go back to serving me faithfully.'

Elijah got into trouble when he forgot his role and started concerning himself with God's role. His role was simply to do what he was told. It was God's role to sustain and secure his own cause. Does this mean that we are to feel no burden at all as we go about the Lord's work? Not at all. It means we must learn to distinguish between the burden that sometimes sighs over the state of the Lord's work and the burden that overwhelms and crushes us with despair. The true balance is to be concerned enough about the cause of God that we are busily at work for him, but not so concerned that we are depressed and melancholy.

This passage ends, thank God, with Elijah going back to his old pattern of promptly obeying the Lord's commands. Assured that the Lord was in complete control of the outcome, Elijah could go back to the struggle with stillness in his heart. May God help all of us who are weary with the struggle to learn the lessons Elijah learned, so that we can continue the struggle with that same stillness in our hearts.

14

The Call of God

So he departed from there, and found Elisha the son of Shaphat, who was ploughing with twelve yoke of oxen before him, and he was with the twelfth. Then Elijah passed by him and threw his mantle on him. And he left the oxen and ran after Elijah, and said, 'Please let me kiss my father and my mother, and then I will follow you.' And he said to him, 'Go back again, for what have I done to you?' So Elisha turned back from him, and took a yoke of oxen and slaughtered them and boiled their flesh, using the oxen's equipment, and gave it to the people, and they ate. Then he arose and followed Elijah, and served him.

1 Kings 19:19–21

In this passage we find Elijah coming down from Mount Horeb to resume his work. His first act was to requisition Elisha for the Lord's work. Does one prophet calling another have anything to do with us? Many would not hesitate to say 'No'. The office of prophet *per se* does not exist today. The prophets were a special class of men to whom God gave special and direct revelation, but now revelation is complete in Scripture and there is, therefore, no more need for this particular office. The modern equivalent to this office is preaching which is bold in its application of the truths of Scripture.

The office to which Elisha was called may be gone, but that in no way makes this passage devoid of relevance. The passage is, after all, not so much about the office of prophet as it is about God calling. And God still calls today. He calls sinners to salvation, and he calls saints to various forms of service.

By studying Elisha's call we can learn some very valuable lessons about the call of God.

1.   *What the Call of God Means.*

Many things could be said at this point, but the primary truth for us to grasp is this—the fact that God calls men means his work is going to go on. As we have already seen, this is a truth that we constantly need to rehearse in our minds. We are living in a time of rampant, militant paganism, and it is very easy for us to begin to wonder if the cause of God is going to survive. This was Elijah's trouble. From his limited perspective the cause of God had dwindled and deteriorated to the point that it was in real jeopardy. As far as he could tell he was the only one left.

On Mount Horeb the Lord showed Elijah that his cause was not lost. He still had plenty of instruments at his disposal. There, God commanded him to anoint three of these instruments (verses 15-17), and he also let Elijah in on a little secret—there were seven thousand faithful ones in Israel who had not bowed the knee to Baal (verse 18).

The command to anoint Elisha had special significance for Elijah. What God said on Mount Horeb was most reassuring and encouraging, but the actual experience of requisitioning Elisha had to be even more comforting to Elijah. Elisha was flesh and blood proof that God's work was not going to end with Elijah, but was going to be carried on. It is very significant that this is the only time in the Bible that a provision was made for a prophet to be anointed. Priests were always anointed and so were kings, but the prophet was usually commissioned directly by God without anyone else being involved. By using Elijah to call and anoint Elisha, the Lord was telling Elijah that he was only an instrument, and God is not in any way dependent upon any of the instruments he chooses. God uses one instrument for his purpose and then he picks up another instrument and uses it. As many have pointed out, God changes workers but the work goes on!

What an encouragement and comfort this is! No matter how bleak the times are, we may rest assured that God's cause will not fail. In every generation he has appointed his instruments to carry his work forward.

2.   *How the Call of God Should be Answered.*

We can sum it all up in two words—willingly and joyfully. Elisha had to be willing to sacrifice much to answer this call. He was busily engaged in plowing when Elijah found him. The fact that he was plowing with twelve yoke of oxen indicates his father was a very wealthy man. Elisha was not only enjoying the wealth of his father at that time but stood to receive quite an inheritance. He was set for life. The life of the prophet was, on the other hand, far from 'cushy'. The prophet had few of the world's goods and was often the object of hostility and outright persecution. Elijah himself had been the subject of an intense manhunt for more than three years.

In addition to all of that, Elisha did not at this point take up prophesying. It is noteworthy that nothing is said about Elijah anointing Elisha immediately, only that he threw his mantle over him. Evidently, the actual anointing of Elisha came later. What, then, was the meaning of Elijah throwing his mantle upon Elisha? It was first a call simply to be Elijah's servant. Notice how this passage ends: 'Then he arose and followed Elijah, and served him.' When Elisha finally began his ministry he was well known as the one who 'pour watered on the hands of Elijah' (2 Kings 3:11).

It is clear that Elisha understood all of this and willingly accepted it. A call to menial service before undertaking the rigours of prophesying! We would not be surprised to read that Elisha said, 'Thanks, but no thanks,' when Elijah's mantle fell around his shoulders. Or to read of him entering into a few negotiations before answering the call: 'Yes, Elijah, I'll go if you guarantee that I will not be put into any dangerous situations and that I will get all holidays off.' But there was no discussion or debate. When the outer call came in the form of Elijah's mantle, the Spirit of God issued an inner call in Elisha's heart and he immediately responded: 'Please let me kiss my father and my mother, and then I will follow you' (verse 20). Elijah permitted Elisha to do this by saying in effect: 'I have not done anything to you which would prevent you from doing this.'

This request and Elijah's response have troubled careful students of the Bible, for they seem to contradict the teaching of Jesus in Luke 9:61-62. There, we find a man who volunteered to follow Jesus but first wanted to return home and say farewell to those at his house. But Jesus' reply was that, 'No one, having put his hand to the plow, and looking back, is fit

100

for the kingdom of God.' So why was it acceptable for Elisha to bid farewell to his family but unacceptable for this man to do the same? The answer has to lie within the hearts of the two men. Elijah knew Elisha's request came from a heart that was eager to follow, while Jesus knew this other man's request came from a heart which was reluctant to follow. To go home and bid farewell was for Elisha the way to show he was making a radical break with his old life and giving himself to his new task. That is why, in the process of bidding farewell, he actually slaughtered a team of oxen and barbecued them on a bonfire. He was finished with that life. The man with whom Jesus was dealing, however, was undoubtedly one whose request came from a desire to return home to discuss and deliberate with his family over whether he was doing the right thing. He had obviously not yet been seized by the same spirit which gripped Elisha—the spirit of willingness to sacrifice for the sake of the call.

Does this mean all Christians should give up all secular employment and devote themselves wholly to serving the Lord? No. Each child of God has a unique calling and each calling carries its own unique demands. What God wants is for each of his children to sacrifice to the point of fulfilling the demands of his particular calling. Being a Sunday School teacher, for instance, does not require one to forsake secular employment, but it does involve sacrificing enough time to study adequately and to minister to the class members. Unfortunately, many Christians today seem more like the man Jesus repudiated than like Elisha. Somewhere along the line we got the idea that Christianity means God does everything for us and we have to do nothing for him. We are content to serve him, so long as it does not interfere with any of our plans or pleasures; but the idea of making a radical sacrifice for the sake of God's kingdom is utterly foreign to us.

Many argue, in effect, that to attract people into our churches Christianity should be made easy and convenient. There must be no talk about giving money, time or talents. Neither can there be any talk about the cardinal tenets of the faith because people today are uninterested in anything that smacks of doctrine. The kind of Christianity these people want is light, breezy and entertaining with short messages filled with jokes and good humour on how to cope with some practical problem. What should our response be to this approach? We must say loudly and clearly that God does not exist for our personal convenience and the church is not like the hamburger chain which urges us to 'have it your way'. Christianity is a body of truth that God has revealed, and coming to grips with this truth means sacrifice and commitment on our part. If we are not willing to sacrifice anything for Christ, we may rest assured we have not really come to know him.

We, like Elijah and Elisha, live in dark and troubling days. In such a day it is very easy for Christians to become discouraged and despondent. The call of Elisha gives us the proper balance for facing this age. On one hand, it tells us not to fret because God's cause is going to triumph. On the other hand, it tells us not to sit idly by but be wholeheartedly and sacrificially involved in God's work.

15

When the Government and the Godly Collide

And it came to pass after these things that Naboth the Jezreelite had a vineyard which was in Jezreel, next to the palace of Ahab king of Samaria. So Ahab spoke to Naboth, saying, 'Give me your vineyard, that I may have it for a vegetable garden, because it is near, next to my house; and for it I will give you a vineyard better than it. Or, if it seems good to you, I will give you its worth in money.' And Naboth said to Ahab, 'The LORD forbid that I should give the inheritance of my fathers to you!' So Ahab went into his house sullen and displeased because of the word which Naboth the Jezreelite had spoken to him; for he had said, 'I will not give you the inheritance of my fathers.' And he lay down on his bed, and turned away his face, and would eat no food. But Jezebel his wife came to him, and said to him, 'Why is your spirit so sullen that you eat no food?' So he said to her, 'Because I spoke to Naboth the Jezreelite, and said to him, "Give me your vineyard for money; or else, if it pleases you, I will give you another vineyard for it." And he answered, "I will not give you my vineyard."' Then Jezebel his wife said to him, 'You now exercise authority over Israel! Arise and eat food, and let your heart be cheerful; I will give you the vineyard of Naboth the Jezreelite.' So she wrote letters in Ahab's name, sealed them with his seal, and sent the letters to the elders and the nobles who were dwelling in the city with Naboth. And she wrote in the letters, saying, 'Proclaim a fast, and seat Naboth with high honor among the people; and seat two men, scoundrels, before him to bear witness against him, saying, "You have blasphemed God and the king." Then take him out, and stone him, that he may die.' So the men of his city, the elders and nobles who were inhabitants of his city, did as Jezebel had sent to them, as it was written in the letters which she had sent to them. They proclaimed a fast, and seated Naboth with high honor among the people. And two men, scoundrels, came in and sat before him; and the scoundrels witnessed against him, against Naboth, in the presence of the people, saying, 'Naboth has blasphemed God and the king!' Then they took him outside the city and stoned him with stones, so that he died. Then they sent to Jezebel, saying, 'Naboth has been stoned and is dead.' And it came to pass, when Jezebel heard that Naboth had been stoned and was dead, that Jezebel said to Ahab, 'Arise, take possession of the vineyard of Naboth the Jezreelite, which he refused to give you for money; for Naboth is not alive, but dead.' So it was, when Ahab heard that Naboth was dead, that Ahab got up and went down to take possession of the vineyard of Naboth the Jezreelite..

1 Kings 21:1-16

H ere we have a most unsavoury story. A man was thrust into a situation where he had to choose between obeying his God and pleasing the state. He chose his God and was murdered by his government.

His name was Naboth. From all indications he was an ordinary, decent, honest, hard-working man—the stuff from which strong nations are made. He happened to possess a vineyard next to the king's property in Jezreel, a vineyard which had been handed down from his fathers. There is something terribly satisfying and delightful about working the same land your fathers worked. It gives a sense of continuity and belonging, of stability and serenity. Never in his wildest dreams did Naboth ever imagine that the vineyard he so proudly possessed would be the cause of his death.

The calm tranquillity of Naboth's life was horribly shattered one day. King Ahab strolled over and said: 'Give me your vineyard.' Ahab knew better! The law of God said landowners were not to sell or trade the land originally allotted to their fathers except in cases of dire poverty (*Lev.* 25:14, 15, 23, 25; *Num.* 36:7). It was the king's job to rule over the people on behalf of God and in accordance with his laws, but Ahab did not care about God's laws. All he cared about was his own comfort and pleasure. So when Naboth refused to give, sell or trade his vineyard, Ahab, behaving more like a spoiled brat than a king, went to his room to sulk and pout.

He didn't sulk long. His wife, Jezebel, believed her husband had the right to choose to do whatever he wanted without regard to anyone else. So she first chided him for being so weak and allowing Naboth to get the better of him, and then she set about to secure the vineyard for Ahab. She arranged to have two 'scoundrels', men without conscience, to testify that Naboth had blasphemed God and the king. It is a perverse irony that the very woman who had worked so feverishly to rid the nation of the knowledge of the true God now accuses Naboth of blaspheming that God.

The plan worked to perfection. Naboth was found guilty and dragged out of the city and stoned. Naboth lost his life and Ahab got his vineyard. It is the job of government to protect its citizens and see to it that each one receives justice. Naboth's government not only failed to protect him from oppression but actually perpetrated the oppression. This appalling episode came hard on the heels of another of Ahab's gross failures. He had the chance to protect his citizens from the murderous Syrian king, Benhadad, by executing him; but instead he treated him as though he were a long lost friend (20:31-43). What a strange and twisted man Ahab was! He protected the man he was supposed to execute and executed the man he was supposed to protect!

But what does all this have to do with us? In the first place, it reminds us that governments often do collide with the godly. It happened to Moses. Although he was brought up in Pharaoh's family and educated in the best schools of Egypt, there came a time when he had to identify himself with his enslaved nation, Israel, and demand that Pharaoh let them go.

It also happened to Daniel and his three friends, Meshach, Shadrach, and Abed-nego. Taken captive from their homeland to live in Babylon, they were under intense pressure to turn their backs on their religious training. On one occasion, they were offered food forbidden by their law, but they refused to eat. Then Daniel's three friends were told to bow down to Nebuchadnezzar's image or be thrown into a fiery furnace. Into the fire they went! And, because of God's power, out they came as good as new! Some years later Daniel found himself in a similar predicament. The king decreed that he alone was to be worshipped for a period of thirty days. Daniel refused to obey and had to spend a night with some very hungry lions!

The apostles and the early church underwent the same experience. Told by the authorities to stop preaching in the name of Jesus, they responded: 'Whether it is right in the sight of God to listen to you more than to God, you judge. For we cannot but speak the things which we have seen and heard' (*Acts* 4:19-20). The experience of the apostles was just a harbinger of things to come. For several years Christians were subject to severe persecution for their faith. When given the opportunity to renounce Jesus and to affirm that Caesar was Lord, they refused to do so and were thrown to the lions or cast into pots of boiling oil.

In the light of all these episodes, it should come as no surprise to find ourselves at tension with the government. Christians do not like to be at tension with their government or with anybody else. There is nothing the Christian desires more than to live peaceably with all men, but there comes a time when the Christian has to oppose his government. What time is that? The experience of Naboth clearly reveals the point at which the government and the godly collide.

Naboth's problem with Ahab was not merely a matter of two strong personalities conflicting, but a matter of radically different and diametrically opposed absolutes trying to occupy the same place at the same time. The absolute at work in Naboth's life, the standard by which he lived and made his choices, was objective in nature—the written Word of God. The absolute at work in Ahab's life was, on the other hand, subjective in nature—whatever brought him pleasure at any particular moment. The absolutes at work in this episode were unnegotiable and totalitarian. Neither could tolerate the other. A collision was inevitable. When Ahab walked into Naboth's vineyard that day with an absolute that says, 'Me first', he found Naboth standing there with an absolute that says, 'God first'. Something had to give!

But what does all this have to do with us? Many seem to be blissfully ignorant of it, but the truth is that Christians are right now, like Naboth, facing a clash of absolutes. There's an ungodly Ahab standing before us and saying: 'Give me your vineyard!' Can we give this modern Ahab a name? Yes, it is secular humanism. It is secular in that it believes this life is all there is or all that matters, and it is humanistic because it asserts that our values should be formed and our lives lived without reference to God. By virtue of these basic tenets, then, secular humanism is radically opposed to and unalterably hostile to biblical Christianity.

Why not just try for peaceful co-existence with secular humanism? That would be fine except for one thing—the secular humanists have an agenda which, if enacted, would put Christians into direct conflict with their government. They are struggling to influence legislation which would threaten the health of the church and attack the moral principles of God's laws. We must be alert to this contemporary Ahab and strain every sinew so that in the affairs of government, as in every area of life, God is given his rightful place. We need to examine ourselves closely and thoroughly. Can we say we fully subscribe to Naboth's standard? Are we clear on the fact that the Christian is one who is obligated to live under the authority of God's Word? Do we understand that when the Bible speaks on an issue that issue is settled for the Christian? This, by the way, is a good way for us to determine whether we really belong to Jesus Christ. If we are content to live under the authority of God's Word, we have every reason to believe we belong to God; but if we are always trying to get around the teachings of God's Word so we can embrace the popular views of the day, we have reason to be deeply concerned about whether we truly know God at all.

We should also cry out mightily to God to send a spiritual

awakening to our nation. The ultimate answer to the steady drift and deterioration of Western societies is not to be found in politics and petitions, but in the power of God.

Finally, even though the days are dark and evil we must not despair. As we shall see, when the government and the godly collide, God sees and knows all about it and will eventually vindicate the godly. That does not mean that each individual Christian is going to emerge from the battle unmarked and unscathed—Naboth lost his life—but it does mean that God's cause is not going to fail and even if we perish in the battle here, we will be forever safe in his arms.

16

Sin Does Not Pay

So it was, when Ahab heard that Naboth was dead, that Ahab got up and went down to take possession of the vineyard of Naboth the Jezreelite. Then the word of the LORD came to Elijah the Tishbite, saying, 'Arise, go down to meet Ahab king of Israel, who lives in Samaria. There he is, in the vineyard of Naboth, where he has gone down to take possession of it. You shall speak to him, saying, "Thus says the LORD: 'Have you murdered and also taken possession?'" And you shall speak to him, saying, "Thus says the LORD: 'In the place where dogs licked the blood of Naboth, dogs shall lick your blood, even yours.'"' Then Ahab said to Elijah, 'Have you found me, O my enemy!' And he answered, 'I have found you, because you have sold yourself to do evil in the sight of the LORD: "Behold, I will bring calamity on you. I will take away your posterity, and will cut off from Ahab every male in Israel, both bond and free. I will make your house like the house of Jeroboam the son of Nebat, and like the house of Baasha the son of Ahijah, because of the provocation with which you have provoked Me to anger, and made Israel sin." And concerning Jezebel the LORD also spoke, saying, "The dogs shall eat Jezebel by the wall of Jezreel." The dogs shall eat whoever belongs to Ahab and dies in the city, and the birds of the air shall eat whoever dies in the field.' But there was no one like Ahab who sold himself to do wickedness in the sight of the LORD, because Jezebel his wife stirred him up. And he behaved very abominably in following idols, according to all that the Amorites had done, whom the LORD had cast out before the children of Israel. So it was, when Ahab heard these words, that he tore his clothes and put on sackcloth on his body, and fasted and lay in sackcloth, and went about mourning. And the word of the LORD came to Elijah the Tishbite, saying, 'See how Ahab has humbled himself before Me? I will not bring the calamity in his days; but in the days of his son I will bring the calamity on his house.'

1 Kings 21:16-29

The story of Ahab's seizure of Naboth's vineyard is a composite picture of a dilemma which has severely tested the faith of God's people down through the years. We see Jezebel writing her diabolical letters and we wonder: 'Where is God? Is he going to let her get away with this sin?' We see the elders of Jezreel reading the letters and making their plans to try Naboth and we ask: 'Where is God? Is he going to ignore such a thing?' We see the false witnesses give their malicious testimony in the sham trial and we shout: 'Where is God? Is he going to let this sin pass?' We see Naboth dragged out of the city where stones are hurled upon him until he is beaten bloody and senseless and we cry: 'Where is God? Is he going to let this outrage stand?' We see Ahab on his way to his new vineyard and we shriek: 'Where is God? Has he decided to let sin pay?'

Does sin pay? That is the question that firmly lodges itself in our minds as we read the first half of this chapter. And the answer seems to be: 'Yes, sin pays! Naboth is dead; Jezebel is cackling in fiendish glee; Ahab is riding smugly to Jezreel and God has neither spoken nor stepped in.'

Ahab had packaged himself up and handed himself entirely over to sin (verse 25). He sinned constantly, diligently, by day and by night, and he seems to have got away completely scot-free. The word 'seems' is the crucial one—nobody ever gets away with sin. The Bible says: 'be sure your sin will find you out' (*Num.* 32:23). In the verses before us, the other foot falls and we find the truth of that verse powerfully demonstrated. This passage reveals three terrible consequences of sin, consequences which are so devastating and depressing that only a fool could read them and still insist sin pays.

1. *Sin Disturbs Our Peace.*

Ahab probably expected the vineyard of Naboth to be a source of great and lasting pleasure to him. It was not. The only pleasure Ahab got out of that vineyard was probably limited to the time it took him to ride there in his chariot. That journey could well have been filled with a warm glow of satisfaction over having got his way and with all kinds of plans for what he would do with the vineyard. But no sooner is he in the vineyard than he hears a rustling among the leaves of the grapevines. He turns to see if one of his servants has followed him but sees instead a familiar figure. The mere sight of that figure must have caused Ahab's heart to fall into his shoes. The prophet, Elijah, had come to the vineyard.

Elijah dispensed with any courtesies and went straight to the reason for his being there. God had sent him with a message. Because Ahab had sold himself to do evil in the sight of God, the dogs of Jezreel would lick his blood just as they had Naboth's, all his male descendants would be cut off, and Jezebel herself would be eaten by the dogs by the wall of Jezreel. Ahab's pleasurable contemplation of his ill-gotten gains was instantly shattered. He would have had little to do with that vineyard and with Jezreel from then on. If the dogs of Jezreel were to lick his blood, he had better stay away from Jezreel. You can imagine Ahab making one excuse after another for not going to Jezreel. From the moment Elijah spoke these words, there was no happiness for Ahab in Jezreel.

So it is with us and our sins. Sin always promises to bring great and lasting pleasures, but it never does. There is pleasure in sin, but the pleasure is momentary and fleeting. The disturbing guilt of sin is lasting. Sin always holds out a pleasant vineyard to entice us, but it never mentions the Elijah who comes with the vineyard—an Elijah to gaze solemnly into our hearts and to declare boldly that God's judgement will ultimately fall on our sins.

2. *Sin Distorts Our Thinking.*

When Ahab saw Elijah he immediately cried out: 'Have you found me, O my enemy?' (verse 20). This was not the first time Ahab had greeted Elijah in this bitter way. When Elijah finally appeared to Ahab after three-and-a-half years of drought, the first words out of Ahab's mouth were: 'Is that you, O troubler of Israel?' (*1 Kings* 18:17). These greetings demonstrate how twisted Ahab's thinking was. He regarded the prophet of God as his enemy, and he regarded that painted, poisonous viper of a wife as his friend.

In reality, Elijah was the best friend Ahab ever had and Jezebel was his greatest enemy. It was Elijah who had the courage to tell Ahab the truth about himself and about God: that he would be blessed if he obeyed God and cursed if he disobeyed Him. Jezebel, on the other hand, constantly 'stirred' Ahab up to do evil (verse 25). She coaxed and cajoled him away from the God of Israel to her god, Baal. She insisted he could turn his back on God with impunity and could secure both peace and prosperity from Baal. Even though Ahab was given overwhelming reasons for serving the true God, Jezebel's hold on him was so powerful that he refused to bow the knee to Jehovah.

It is easy for us to read of Ahab and shake our heads in rueful amazement over his blindness. Few seem to realize how sin continues to deceive and distort. How many become offended when a preacher says all are sinners and stand guilty before a holy God! How many accuse the preacher of being negative when he insists something must be done about our sins or we will perish! How many dismiss the preacher as hopelessly dogmatic and narrow when he says Jesus Christ is the only way of salvation! How few realize that the preacher who proclaims such truths is the greatest friend anyone could possibly have! The true enemy of the sinner is the preacher who lulls him to sleep by making him believe sin is not serious, God is not holy, and judgement is not real.

We would not regard the doctor as our enemy if he were to tell us we have a dreadful disease, but would properly think he is trying to help us. If we were out sailing, we would not blame a lighthouse for showing us where the treacherous rocks are. Why should we blame preachers for telling us those truths that are plainly revealed in God's Word? The apostle Paul asked the Galatians: 'Have I therefore become your enemy because I you the truth?' (*Gal.* 4:16). It is tragic that so many faithful preachers have, like Paul, been made to feel as if they were the enemies of God's people.

3. *Sin Finally Destroys Everything.*

Sin destroyed Ahab just as Elijah had warned. Try as he may he could not keep the prophecy from coming true. In a battle at Ramoth Gilead, Ahab removed his royal robes and donned his armour. All his precautions were to no avail. A Syrian soldier drew a bow at random and the arrow struck Ahab between the joints of his armour, and he died.

That evening, someone took his chariot to the pool of Samaria to wash the blood out of it, and there the dogs came and licked his blood, just as Elijah had predicted (*1 Kings* 22:29-38). Some critics have argued that Elijah's prophecy was not completely fulfilled. It specifically stated that the dogs would lick Ahab's blood in the place where they licked Naboth's blood. That was at Jezreel, but Scripture says they licked Ahab's blood at 'a pool of Samaria'. But in all probability this pool was actually in Jezreel, and the servants of Ahab stopped there on the way to Samaria and washed out the chariot before continuing to Samaria to bury the king.

Sin also destroyed all the male descendants of Ahab (Jehu and others saw to that (*2 Kings* 9:24-26; 10:6-7, 9-17)) and it finally destroyed Jezebel herself. Her own servants pushed her out of the window as she watched Jehu come through the city gate, and she was trampled by his chariot. When he sent someone back to bury her, the dogs had already savaged her body. Nothing was left except her skull, her feet and the palms of her hands. No one has ever stated better the significance of this than R.G. Lee in his famous sermon, *Pay Day—Some Day:* 'God Almighty saw to it that the hungry dogs despised the brains that conceived the plot that took Naboth's life. God Almighty saw to it that the mangy lean dogs of the back alleys despised the hands that wrote the plot that took Naboth's life. God Almighty saw to that the lousy dogs which ate carrion despised the feet that walked in Baal's courts and then in Naboth's vineyard.'[7]

What should we learn from sin's complete destruction of Ahab and his family? We could dismiss all of this as simply meaningless ancient history if sin had died with Ahab, but it did not. Sin is just as much a part of our nature as it was his. We may not have outwardly sinned as deeply as he but, make no mistake, we are sinners just the same (*Rom.* 3:10-23). And because we are sinners we stand under God's condemnation. Sin ultimately cost Ahab his life, but it cost him far more than that. The Bible says the godless perish in eternal destruction.

Thank God, there is a solution. God himself has provided it in his Son, the Lord Jesus Christ. If we come to him in true repentance and faith, our sins will be forgiven and the sentence of divine wrath will be lifted. If you have not received Jesus Christ as your Lord and Saviour, bow before him now, for there is no other provision for sin.

---

7   Robert G. Lee, *Pay Day—Some Day*, Zondervan Publishing Company, Grand Rapids, Michigan, 1957, p. 31.

17

'Phoney Repentance', Abundant Mercy

So it was, when Ahab heard these words, that he tore his clothes and put on sackcloth on his body, and fasted and lay in sackcloth, and went about mourning. And the word of the LORD came to Elijah the Tishbite, saying, 'See how Ahab has humbled himself before Me? I will not bring the calamity in his days; but in the days of his son I will bring the calamity on his house.'

1 Kings 21:27-29

One of the major problems of the church today is 'phoney repentance'. Multitudes have walked down the aisle, mouthed the right words, and joined the church only to become what is delicately called 'inactive members'. All kinds of explanations have been offered for this sad state of affairs. Some attribute the problem to ineptness in 'follow up'. They argue that these inactive members came to church really wanting to serve the Lord, but no one told them how to go about it and they became discouraged and dropped out. Others say the problem is due to failing to teach new converts about a second level of Christian living. Often, we are told, we simply tell people to accept Jesus as Saviour and we fail to tell them they must also accept him as Lord. Many, therefore, have settled down in something of a halfway house. They are not lost, but neither are they living for the Lord. They are, the argument goes, 'carnal Christians'—saved, but living as unbelievers live.

The common assumption in both of these explanations is that those who have made a profession of faith are genuinely saved. Very few seem willing to allow the possibility that many of our 'inactive members' have simply never truly come to know God at all; that their repentance was superficial and incomplete; and that, therefore, they remain in their sins.

The reluctance to talk about phoney conversions is surprising, because Scripture has so much to say on the subject. There are, for instance, the teachings of Jesus: in the Sermon on the Mount, he explicitly warned about the danger of being deceived on our standing with God (*Matt.* 7:21-23); in his parable of the sower, he spoke about the 'stony ground' hearer who receives the word with joy but in whom the word does not take root (*Matt.* 13:20-21). In addition, we have clear warnings from Paul (*2 Cor.* 13:5), Peter (*2 Pet.* 1:10-11), John (*1 John* 2:18-19; 5:13), and the author of the Epistle to the

Hebrews (6:4-6; 10:26-39) on the danger of being deceived about being converted.

We also have several notable examples of spurious conversions. The names of Esau (*Heb.* 12:16-17), Judas Iscariot (*Acts* 1:16-20), Simon Magus (*Acts* 8:9-24), and Demas (*2 Tim.* 4:10) are all inextricably linked to 'phoney repentance'. And here in the Old Testament we have the case of Ahab. As hard as it may be to believe, this passage says Ahab, upon hearing Elijah's message of judgement, tore his clothes, put on sackcloth, fasted, and went about mourning. It also tells us that because of this self-humiliation, God delayed sending the promised judgement.

Many would have no doubt that these verses tell us that Ahab, the arch-enemy of God and godliness, had a true and genuine conversion experience and lived for the Lord for the rest of his life. Certainly, every child of God would like to believe this. We would all like to see Ahab and Elijah strolling together on heaven's golden streets. Yet even though some of the greatest sinners in history have been plucked out of hell at the very last moment, the evidence is overwhelming that Ahab was not one of them.

Ahab's demonstration of repentance was very striking and impressive, but consider for a moment what he did not do. First, he did nothing to repudiate Jezebel or to reduce her evil influence in the kingdom. Second, he took no action to restore Naboth's vineyard to his heirs or next of kin. Third, he did not break with his idols—when he and Jehoshaphat, king of Judah, decided to go to war against the Syrians, Ahab consulted with four hundred false prophets (*1 Kings* 22:6) If Ahab had been truly converted, it is safe to say that he would have addressed each of these situations, but he did not.

We should also consider what Ahab said after the four hundred false prophets assured him of success in the battle against

Syria but Jehoshaphat asked to hear from 'a prophet of the Lord'. There was such a prophet, Ahab conceded, but 'I hate him because he never prophesies anything good about me, but always bad' (22:7-8). The fact that this prophet, Micaiah, had nothing good to say about Ahab indicates that the king of Israel had not truly repented of his sin; and Ahab's confession of his hatred for a servant of God ought to remove all question about his spiritual condition.

But if Ahab's repentance was not genuine, how are we to explain his tearing his clothes, putting on sackcloth, fasting and mourning? The answer is that these actions were all induced by fear of judgement, not by true sorrow for sin. Ahab knew Elijah extremely well by this time. He knew whatever Elijah said would most certainly come true, and he was distraught because God's judgement was hanging over him and he could not escape it. What could possibly be wrong with Ahab fearing judgement? The Bible says we must all eventually stand before God to give account of ourselves (*Rom.* 14:12; *Heb.* 9:27), and it even warns us to fear him who has the power 'to cast into hell' (*Luke* 12:5). So at first sight it seems somewhat unfair to criticize Ahab for being motivated by the fear of judgement.

Yet the point we must keep in mind is that the Bible tells us about judgement so we will hate our sin and turn from it. Sin is what leads to judgement. Ahab feared judgement but he did not hate his sin. He believed the Word of God but, as we have noted, would not and did not forsake the sin. He wanted to escape judgement while hanging on to his sin—and that cannot be done.

Because Ahab did not truly hate his sin, he resorted to mere outward rituals to stave off the judgement while clinging to sin within his heart. The Lord says it is all right to fast and weep and mourn, as long as these things are done with the whole heart. But if the heart is not broken there is absolutely no point in someone rending their garments (*Joel* 2:12-13). Ahab tore his garments, but his heart was the same as ever.

Many today are in exactly the same position. They believe the Word of God, but they will not do what it prescribes. They believe there is a God, and they believe they must some day stand before him, but they try to prepare for that day by going through the external motions of religion, and not by making a complete break with their sins. How many sit in church each Sunday with the hope that their religious observances will somehow appease God, and all the while they stubbornly refuse to turn from their sins?

But this leaves us with a tricky question. If Ahab's repentance was 'phoney', why did God take note of it and decide to withhold his judgement for a time?

i.   God was simply demonstrating again the greatness of his mercy. The prophet Isaiah tells us judgement is God's 'strange' or 'unusual' act (*Isa.* 28:21), which shows us that God receives no pleasure or delight from judgement. His judgement is always a last resort.

ii.   By delaying Ahab's judgement, God was also giving comfort to all those who read these pages. If God was good enough to spare for a while someone who had, at best, only partially repented, what will he do for the one who sincerely repents? Matthew Henry puts it like this: 'If a pretending partial penitent shall go to his house reprieved, doubtless a sincere penitent shall go to his house justified.'[8] But as much as God delights in showing mercy, he will never compromise his word in order to show mercy. The temporary reprieve given to Ahab did not change one iota God's promise to judge Ahab and his family. The judgement finally came just as God promised.

8   Henry, p. 699.

Jesus' parable of the fig tree perfectly pictures the blend of God's mercy and judgement. In the parable, God is the owner of the fruitless fig tree. Because he is merciful he agrees to give the fig tree another year to bear fruit, but at the end of that year of mercy the fig tree is to be cut down. The message is clear. God's mercy is great, but there is an end to it (*Luke* 13:6-9). Ours is a time in which people seem to come lightly and easily to Christ. Deep knowledge of sin, and sincere sorrow over it are increasingly rare. Churches and preachers are so anxious to gain a following that they willingly accept all professions of faith at face value. How we need to be reminded of Ahab and his phoney repentance! Ahab teaches us two very serious and powerful lessons:

  i. It is possible to go a long way in religion and not be truly converted.

  ii. True repentance will always evidence itself in a change of attitude toward sin and in changed behaviour.

May God help each of us who has made a profession of faith to bring these lessons home to our hearts and to make sure that our profession is the genuine article.

18

The Word of God
Challenged and Confirmed

Moab rebelled against Israel after the death of Ahab. Now Ahaziah fell through the lattice of his upper room in Samaria, and was injured; so he sent messengers and said to them, 'Go, inquire of Baal-Zebub, the god of Ekron, whether I shall recover from this injury.' But the angel of the LORD said to Elijah the Tishbite, 'Arise, go up to meet the messengers of the king of Samaria, and say to them, "Is it because there is no God in Israel that you are going to inquire of Baal-Zebub, the god of Ekron?" Now therefore, thus says the LORD: "You shall not come down from the bed to which you have gone up, but you shall surely die."' So Elijah departed. And when the messengers returned to him, he said to them, 'Why have you come back?' So they said to him, 'A man came up to meet us, and said to us, "Go, return to the king who sent you, and say to him, 'Thus says the LORD: "Is it because there is no God in Israel that you are sending to inquire of Baal-Zebub, the god of Ekron? Therefore you shall not come down from the bed to which you have gone up, but you shall surely die."'"' Then he said to them, 'What kind of man was it who came up to meet you and told you these words?' So they answered, 'He was a hairy man, and wore a leather belt around his waist.' And he said, 'It is Elijah the Tishbite.' Then the king sent to him a captain of fifty with his fifty men. So he went up to him, and there he was, sitting on the top of a hill. And he spoke to him: 'Man of God, the king has said, "Come down!"' So Elijah answered and said to the captain of fifty, 'If I am a man of God, then let fire come down from heaven and consume you and your fifty men.' And fire came down from heaven and consumed him and his fifty. Then he sent to him another captain of fifty with his fifty men. And he answered and said to him: 'Man of God, thus has the king said, "Come down quickly!"' So Elijah answered and said to them, 'If I am a man of God,' let fire come down from heaven and consume you and your fifty men!' And the fire of God came down from heaven and consumed him and his fifty. Again, he sent a third captain of fifty with his fifty men. And the third captain of fifty went up, and came and fell on his knees before Elijah, and pleaded with him, and said to him: 'Man of God,' please let my life and the life of these fifty servants of yours be precious in your sight. Look, fire has come down from heaven and burned up the first two captains of fifties with their fifties. But let my life now be precious in your sight.' And the angel of the LORD said to Elijah, 'Go down with him; do not be afraid of him.' So he arose and went down with him to the king. Then he said to him, 'Thus says the LORD: "Because you have sent messengers to inquire of Baal-Zebub, the god of Ekron, is it because there there is no God in Israel to inquire of His word? Therefore you shall not come down from the bed to which you have gone up, but you shall surely die"' So Ahaziah died according to the word of the LORD which Elijah had spoken.

2 Kings 1:1-17a

This passage of Scripture is one of those which is either vehemently attacked or blissfully ignored. It is not hard to see why. The message of this portion of Scripture is distasteful and unsavoury to the vast majority of people. It says the prophet Elijah twice called fire down from heaven to consume an army captain and his company of fifty men.

Nevertheless, no matter how much we dislike this message we ignore it at our peril, for it pictures an unavoidable truth. It teaches us not to place a mere human word over the Word of God because the Word of God is ultimately going to prevail. The truth is God used temporal judgements such as this to let us know that there is a far worse judgement awaiting those who disregard the Word of God. Jesus, for instance, used two temporal calamities to drive home this truth: 'unless you repent, you will all likewise perish' (*Luke* 13:1-5). We cannot, therefore, dismiss this story about Ahaziah and Elijah but must carefully weigh its truths.

1. *The Word of God is Clearly Delivered (verses 1-8).*
If ever there was a man who should have ordered his life in accordance with the Word of God it was Ahaziah, for he lived in the steady glare of the power and truth of God's Word. He had the written Word of God by which to order his steps, including the writings of Moses in Deuteronomy, which made it as clear as the noonday sun that the people of Israel were to worship the Lord God alone and that the sin of idolatry would not go unpunished.

In addition, Ahaziah had the calamitous example of his father. Ahab disregarded the Word of God and forced Israel to worship Baal, with the result that the nation suffered a devastating famine. Ahaziah not only saw the famine come upon the land just as Elijah had said, but he also saw the famine broken by the word of the same prophet of God. But

Ahaziah also saw Elijah's word fulfilled most painfully in the death of his father. Ahab had violated the Word of God by unlawfully seizing the vineyard of Naboth. God responded to Ahab's sin by again sending Elijah with a message of devastating judgement, and Ahaziah knew that the dogs of Jezreel had completely fulfilled Elijah's prophecy by licking up the blood of his father.

Surely Ahaziah would be intelligent enough scrupulously to obey the Word of God after having seen the terrible consequences of idolatry and disobedience. Perhaps we can even hear him saying: 'If there is anything I have learned it is not to do what my father did!' Yet incredibly, Ahaziah learned nothing. The Bible tells us that upon assuming his father's throne, Ahaziah 'served Baal and worshipped him, and provoked the LORD God of Israel to anger, according to all that his father had done' (*1 Kings* 22:53).

God would have been justified in sending judgement upon Ahaziah without a single word of warning, but he is gracious, kind and long-suffering. In Ahaziah's case, God spoke in three distinct ways:

i.   *The nation of Moab rebelled against Ahaziah.*
David had subjugated the Moabites and for a great number of years they had paid tribute to Israel. During the reign of Ahaziah, however, Moab rebelled.

ii. *Ahaziah suffered a fall and was seriously injured.*
The new king of Israel was suddenly faced with national and personal troubles. Were they simply matters of coincidence? Some might be inclined to think so, but the truth is that God uses our circumstances to get our attention. Ahaziah already had the written word of God and the example of his father, now he was experiencing harsh adversity in his own life. We are most truly ourselves at such times of trial and painful difficulty, and how we react to adversity is a wonderful meas-

ure of our nature, character and spiritual state. How did Ahaziah react? Did he turn to God and do his will? Far from it. Instead he sent messengers to the god of Ekron, Baal-Zebub, to see if he would recuperate from his injuries.

iii. *Elijah told the messengers to return to Ahaziah with the word that he would not recuperate but would die (verse 4).*

As the messengers made their way to Baal-Zebub they were met by the prophet Elijah. Through Elijah, God spoke to Ahaziah in a third distinct way and, in so doing, gave him one last chance to bow to the Word of God. This sounds like a harsh, unkind message, but in reality it was a word of grace to the king. Some people never have the opportunity to prepare for death, but this word gave Ahaziah that opportunity.

2. *The Word of God is Challenged and Defied (verses 9-12).*

The Word of God has never sounded more frequently and more clearly than it did in Ahaziah's case, yet even on his deathbed and presented with a final opportunity to bow before it, the king challenged and defied Jehovah. He was infuriated by Elijah's message and sent a captain out with fifty men to capture the prophet. Essentially, he was saying: 'I don't like the message so I am going to destroy the messenger.' The pride and stupidity of this man almost beggars belief. Did he not realize that Elijah spoke for God? How could he fail to recognize that his trouble was not with Elijah but with Elijah's God? How could he be so deluded as to believe that by destroying Elijah he could destroy God?

We may shake our heads in bemusement at Ahaziah's reaction to Elijah's message, but many of us have done or are doing exactly the same thing. The 'Ahaziah syndrome' lives on in everyone who tries to deny or destroy God's message. The spirit of Ahaziah is alive and well in all those who have been given clear demonstrations of God's power and truth but who so resent it that they try to escape by going to another church. That syndrome is also alive and well in all those who stay in their Bible-preaching church but carry a bitter, resentful attitude toward God's messenger.

Ahaziah's attempt to silence the Word of God met with devastating results. When the first captain and his company found Elijah the captain said: 'Man of God, the king has said, "Come down!"' (verse 9). If we are to understand what was going on here we have to put the emphasis on those four little words 'the king has said'. Elijah had spoken and now the king was speaking. Elijah had spoken the Word of God to the king and now the king was speaking his own word to Elijah. The king pitted his word against the Word of God, seeking, as it were, to silence God.

We see exactly the same thing today. Any minister will tell you how commonly he hears statements like: 'Yes, I know the Bible says such and such but I believe such and such'; and, 'Yes, I know the Bible says such and such, but times are different now.' The common denominator in all such statements is the placing of the person's own word or own thoughts over the authority of the Word of God. Every time we or anybody else does this, we say with Ahaziah: 'The Word of God must be silenced.'

No sooner had this first captain put the word of the king above the Word of God than Elijah shot back: 'If I am a man of God, then let fire come down from heaven and consume you and your fifty men.' (v. 10). Immediately, fire fell from heaven and the captain and his company were destroyed. In this terrible event, Ahaziah received yet another indication of the truth of the Word of God, yet he still steadfastly refused to bow to the will of God. How hard the human heart is by nature. When word reached him about the death of the first company of men, Ahaziah simply sent out another captain with another fifty soldiers. Again he pitted his word against the Word of God and again he lost. The second captain and his fifty men were consumed in exactly the same way as the others.

These two episodes have caused considerable consternation and perplexity for many children of God. We would have no trouble if it had been the king himself who had confronted Elijah and suffered this fate. We know how extremely wicked he was, and had he been consumed by fire we would say he got what he so richly deserved. But why did God consume these captains and their men? It could be that these men were completely in sympathy with their king and had nothing but resentment and hostility toward the prophet and his God. We know the godly had dwindled to a small number during Ahab's reign, and we should not be surprised, therefore, if all these men deserved this judgement.

But even if this were not the case, there is no need for us to balk at the idea of God's judgement falling on men who were not sympathetic to the king. If there is anything written large in human history, it is the fact that our choices always affect those around us. If we choose wickedness, we should not be surprised to see the effects of wickedness touch our families and friends. Some who profess to be shocked and scandalized by God sending fire upon these poor soldiers need to see that the problem was not God's judgement but the king's wickedness. That was what brought calamity on his soldiers. It is a solemn and important lesson—our wickedness may well bring calamity on those around us.

3. *The Word of God is Embraced and Vindicated (verses 13-17a).*
After the second band of soldiers was consumed we might expect that Ahaziah would finally have recognized the futility of his power. But he remained just as adamant and just as stubborn, and sent yet another captain with another fifty men.

However, when this captain finally encountered Elijah, he approached him in an entirely different way. He said nothing about the word of the king. The officer knew what had happened to his predecessors and knew that the word of the king was meaningless and powerless—what counted was the Word of God. He recognised that the Word of God cannot be successfully challenged or defied, but must be embraced and accepted, so he did not try to pit the word of the king against it as the others had done. Instead, he bowed before Elijah and pleaded for his own life and the lives of those who were with him—and this captain and his band were spared.

At this point, the Lord assured Elijah that Ahaziah would do nothing more to harm him and that he should accompany the company of soldiers back to the king. Once in the king's presence, the prophet delivered again the word he had delivered from the beginning: namely, that Ahaziah would not recover from his injuries. The very next statement says: 'So Ahaziah died, according to the word of the Lord which Elijah had spoken' (verse 17).

This passage is no mere myth or legend. Neither does it tell us about a God who no longer exists. It is full of sober truth for each of us, calling us to examine our attitude toward the Word of God. Are we guilty of defying it as Ahaziah did and of pitting our thoughts and words against it; or, like the third captain, have we bowed in submission to it? We may rest assured that the Word of God is going to be confirmed and vindicated. There is absolutely nothing we can do to change that. The only thing which can be changed is our attitude toward God's truth. The question now is, will we change it?

19

The Cause of God Then and Now

And it came to pass, when the LORD was about to take up Elijah into heaven by a whirlwind, that Elijah went with Elisha from Gilgal. Then Elijah said to Elisha, 'Stay here, please, for the LORD has sent me on to Bethel.' And Elisha said, 'As the LORD lives, and as your soul lives, I will not leave you!' So they went down to Bethel. And the sons of the prophets who were at Bethel came out to Elisha, and said to him, 'Do you know that the LORD will take away your master from over you today?' And he said, 'Yes, I know; keep silent!' Then Elijah said to him, 'Elisha, stay here, please, for the LORD has sent me on to Jericho.' And he said, 'As the LORD lives, and as your soul lives, I will not leave you!' So they came to Jericho. And the sons of the prophets who were at Jericho came to Elisha and said to him, 'Do you know that the LORD will take away your master from over you today?' So he answered, 'Yes, I know; keep silent!' Then Elijah said to him, 'Stay here, please, for the LORD has sent me on to the Jordan.' And he said, 'As the LORD lives, and as your soul lives, I will not leave you!' So the two of them went on. And fifty men of the sons of the prophets went and stood facing them at a distance, while the two of them stood by the Jordan. Now Elijah took his mantle, rolled it up,

---

and struck the water; and it was divided this way and that, so that the two of them crossed over on dry ground. And so it was, when they had crossed over, that Elijah said to Elisha, 'Ask! What may I do for you, before I am taken away from you?' And Elisha said, 'Please let a double portion of your spirit be upon me.' So he said, 'You have asked a hard thing,. Nevertheless, if you see me when I am taken from you, it shall be so for you; but if not, it shall not be so.' Then it happened, as they continued on and talked, that suddenly a chariot of fire appeared with horses of fire, and separated the two of them; and Elijah went up by a whirlwind into heaven. Now Elisha saw it, and he cried out, 'My father, my father, the chariot of Israel and its horsemen!' So he saw him no more. And he took hold of his own clothes and tore them into two pieces. He also took up the mantle of Elijah that had fallen from him, and went back and stood by the bank of the Jordan. Then he took the mantle of Elijah that had fallen from him, and struck the water, and said, 'Where is the LORD God of Elijah?' And when he also had struck the water, it was divided this way and that; and Elisha crossed over. Now when the sons of the prophets who were from Jericho saw him, they said, 'The spirit of Elijah rests on Elisha.' And they came to meet him, and bowed to the ground before him.

2 Kings 2:1–15

We live in a time very much like Elijah's, a time in which the cause of God is being fiercely attacked on every side. Such a time always causes some professing Christians completely to abandon their profession. Others begin to renegotiate their faith and seek to make room for the popular beliefs of the day within the framework of Christianity. Still others continue to hold to historic Christianity but do so with a great deal of melancholy and with very little zeal.

The story of Elijah is tremendously encouraging for all Christians who find themselves depressed and despondent with the future of the cause of God. In one of the bleakest times ever experienced by his people, God did three things with Elijah: First, God used him. Second, God preserved him. Third, when the prophet himself despaired over the cause of God, God renewed him. If God did these things with Elijah, who was a 'man with a nature like ours' (*James* 5:17), we can certainly expect him to use, preserve and renew us.

Perhaps no part of Elijah's life is more encouraging than its final hours. Knowing the Lord was about to take him home, Elijah set out from Gilgal to bid farewell to the schools of the prophets at Bethel and Jericho. It was only fitting that the man who had stood so strongly and steadfastly against the raging tide of iniquity give the young prophets a final word of encouragement to be true to the Lord. After visiting these prophets, Elijah and Elisha crossed over the Jordan River, talked for a few minutes, and then Elijah was swept away into glory by horses and a chariot of fire. It was a stunning and fitting end to a stunningly faithful life.

Two great lessons leap out as we consider this glorious event and what led up to it.

1. *We See That God's Cause is Ultimately Going to Prevail.*
As we have already seen many times in this book, Elijah was effectively the very embodiment of the cause of God and the Word of God. This is the reason we find Elijah being used in the New Testament as the representative of all the prophets. The prophets were men who spoke the Word of God, and Elijah was the prototype of all the prophets. So when the horses and chariot of fire swept down from heaven to snatch Elijah away, it was not simply to honour him as a man. It was to demonstrate that what Elijah stood for—the Word of God— was ultimately going to triumph and prevail.

If we were able to hurl ourselves back through time and land in Israel on the day Elijah was taken, then begin to survey the lives and beliefs of the people, we would conclude that it was highly doubtful that the Word of God would prevail. Even though Baal worship had been somewhat slowed by Elijah's stand, it was still dominant throughout the land; Jezebel, its prime promoter, was still alive and fiendishly committed to removing every vestige of God from Israel; the Israelites still worshipped golden calves at shrines in Bethel and Dan; and the nation was filled with oppression of the poor, disregard for justice, a crass craving for material things, and cruel and ruthless violence.

But things are not always as they seem. Many times in the history of mankind it has looked as if the cause of God was on the verge of utter extinction, only to be suddenly and dramatically revived and renewed. And the final vindication of God's cause is going to come in heaven not in this dark world. The sweeping up of Elijah demonstrated that there is more to reality than this world—that there is a heaven that is real, and that at any time the heavenly world can burst in and invade this earth.

So whatever it is that we find so depressing and discouraging today, we must take heart. No matter how bleak this hour is, no matter how heavy the clouds of gloom, God's cause is ultimately going to prevail! There is coming a glad and glorious day in which God's truth will be vindicated and God's people are going to be gathered up as a man gathers his precious jewels (*Mal.* 3:17). On that day, they are going to shine as brightly as the stars of the firmament, and every knee is going to bow and every tongue confess that Jesus Christ is Lord to the glory of God the Father. The church today finds herself in dire straits, but she must take comfort in the words of her Lord: 'I will build My church, and the gates of Hades shall not prevail against it' (*Matt.* 16:18).

The translation of Elijah, then, is a powerful and abiding picture of the triumph which awaits the children of God. It tells us, in no uncertain terms, that we need not despair because God's cause is going to triumph.

2. *We See That God Has a Plan to Preserve His Cause on Earth at the Present Time.*

As glorious and marvellous as the knowledge of the eventual triumph of God's cause is, we are all painfully aware that it is still in the future. We are not there yet. What about the present? What about the cause of God here and now? The events leading up to Elijah's translation teach us that God will preserve his cause in the present through faithful, earnest men. In other words, we are reminded once more that we should not take the fact that God's cause is ultimately going to prevail as an excuse for just sitting back in idleness. Tell some Christians God's cause is going to prevail and they seem to respond: 'Oh, good. That means there's nothing for me to do.'

God not only demonstrated in Elijah's translation that his cause was not going to fail, but also that he had a plan to preserve his cause on the earth at that time. What was his plan?

It was a man named Elisha. He had used Elijah as his instrument and now he was about to use Elisha. Thank God for the truth we have here—God changes instruments but his cause goes on, and the same is true today. But let us note carefully that God does not just use any kind of instrument. As we read this passage, we see that Elisha was a special kind of man with certain distinct traits. God always uses as his instruments those who have certain traits, and if we want to be used by him to help preserve his cause in this generation we need to look diligently at our own lives to see if these traits are present.

The first trait which God looks for is firm resolve. When Elijah set out on his final journey he told Elisha to stay in Gilgal. Elisha refused and joined Elijah on his trip to Bethel. When Elijah got ready to set out from Bethel he told Elisha to stay there, but Elisha again refused and accompanied the prophet to Jericho. When Elijah set out from Jericho he again told Elisha to stay, but again Elisha refused and accompanied him to the Jordan. Can we honestly say that we are people of firm resolve? We need not expect the cause of the Lord to prosper and flourish unless we know this resolve. My assessment is that the Lord's work is flagging today because there is a shortage of Christians with iron-clad commitment. We desire to see the Lord's work flourish, but there is a world of difference between desire and determination. Only the latter will move the cause of God forward.

The second trait which God looks for is a refusal to listen to melancholy counsel. When he and Elijah got ready to leave Bethel the prophets there said to him: 'Do you know that the Lord will take away your master from over you today?' When he and Elijah got ready to leave Jericho, the prophets there said the same thing to him. In each case, Elisha responded by saying: 'Yes, I know; keep silent!' In each case the prophets were getting ready to draw a depressing, melancholy conclusion from the fact that Elijah was about to be taken; but in each case Elisha refused to let them do so. He cut them off before they began their litany of woes: 'What are we going to do after Elijah is gone? What will become of the cause of God now? All is lost!' Elisha knew this type of thing was coming and he refused to listen to it. Similarly, if we expect to be the type of people who are used of God to preserve his cause, we must stop our ears against the kind of pessimism which makes the cause of God seem hopeless, and fill our minds and hearts with the promises of Holy Scripture that God's cause is going to triumph.

The final trait which was in Elisha, and is in all the greatest servants of God, is a fervent, intense yearning for the power and the Spirit of God. When Elisha and Elijah finally got across the Jordan to the place where Elijah was to be taken, the elder prophet asked: 'What may I do for you, before I am taken away from you?' (verse 9). What a great opportunity this was for Elisha. Here was this great man of God giving him a virtual blank cheque—all he, Elisha, had to do was fill in the amount. If you really want to know where you are spiritually, just put yourself in Elisha's shoes for a moment. If you were given the chance to receive whatever you were about to ask, what would you ask for?

There was absolutely no doubt in Elisha's mind about what to ask for: 'Please let a double portion of your spirit be upon me' (verse 9). With the opportunity to ask for what he wished, Elisha asked for the power and the Spirit of God to be upon him in a measure twice that of Elijah. It was not that Elisha wanted to be greater than Elijah, but rather that he so felt his inadequacy and smallness that he knew he would need twice what Elijah had if he were to be a worthy successor of him.

Elisha, then, was a man of firm resolve who refused to listen to the counsel of hopelessness, and a man who was fervently desirous of the power and Spirit of God. These are the very traits we must possess if we are to be used by God in our day. Let us even now take courage in the fact that God's cause is going to triumph, but let us also resolve to be the type of men and women God can use to preserve his cause in the world until that glorious day when his Son, our Lord Jesus Christ, will come again to make a new heaven and a new earth which will last for eternity.

SOME OTHER
BANNER OF TRUTH
TITLES

COME DOWN, LORD!

Roger Ellsworth

Come Down, Lord! is a succinct, readable and biblically-based treatment of the vital theme of revival. Its seven short chapters go directly to the heart of the matter, as their headings indicate: We miss You; We need You; We wait for You; We will meet You; We have wronged You; We belong to You; We beseech You.

Taking as his starting place the widespread absence of the sense of God's holy presence and our need of his grace, Roger Ellsworth traces the profound analysis of the church's spiritual decay outlined in Isaiah 63:3-64:12, and applies its message to our times:

'We have heard for years that if we do not repent of our sins, God will send judgment upon us. We may think we are getting by with sin because things do not appear to be so bad. What most of us do not realize is God's judgment has already set in. Our apathy about spiritual things is God's judgment upon us.'

While calculated to expose our spiritual need, *Come Down, Lord!* will also stimulate repentance, prayer and fresh faith in the promised mercy of God.

ISBN 0 85151 539 8
64pp. Paperback

IS THERE AN ANSWER?

Roger Ellsworth

Most people are vaguely aware of a man named Job who suffered incredible calamities. Few, however, realize how intensely relevant is the Old Testament book that bears his name. Job was asking the very questions many are asking today. It is true, of course, that others are not asking these questions. Their lives are bounded by pursuing material things and indulging themselves with a parade of pleasures. The only interest these people have in these questions is in devising ways studiously to avoid them. But for those who are weary of such a simplistic, superficial diet, this little work will have lasting value. These expositions will also be helpful to Christians who have struggled with these questions and are seeking to help others find answers.

ISBN 0 85151 570 3
32pp. Booklet

THE LIFE OF ELIJAH

A. W. Pink

The life of Elijah has gripped the thought and imagination of preachers and writers in all ages. His sudden appearance out of complete obscurity, his dramatic interventions in the national history of Israel, his miracles, his departure from the earth in a chariot of fire all serve to that end. 'He comes in like a tempest, who went out like a whirlwind', says Bishop Hall; 'the first we hear from him is an oath and a threat'. Judgment and mercy were mingled throughout Elijah's astonishing career.

It is fitting that the lessons which may be drawn from Elijah's ministry should be presented afresh to our generation. History repeats itself. The wickedness and idolatry rampant in Ahab's reign live in our gross 20th century's profanities and corruptions. False prophets occupy large spheres of influence and truths dear to our evangelical forefathers have been downtrodden as the mire in the streets. A. W. Pink clearly felt called to the task of smiting the ungodliness of the age with the rod of God's anger while at the same time encouraging the faithful remnant. With these objects he undertakes the exposition of Elijah's ministry and applies it to the contemporary situation.

ISBN 0 85151 041 8
320pp. Paperback

THE SOVEREIGNTY OF GOD

A. W. Pink

'Present day conditions', writes the author, call loudly for a new examination and new presentation of God's omnipotence, God's sufficiency, God's sovereignty. From every pulpit in the land it needs to be thundered forth that God still lives, that God still observes, that God still reigns. Faith is now in the crucible, it is being tested by fire, and there is no fixed and sufficient resting-place for the heart and mind but in *the Throne of God*. What is needed now, as never before, is a full, positive, constructive setting forth of the Godhood of God.

ISBN 0 85151 133 3
160pp. Paperback

PROFITING FROM THE WORD

A. W. Pink

How much profit do we gain from our reading of the Bible? 'All Scripture', we are told in 2 Timothy 3:16, 17, 'is profitable'. But how much do we gain from our reading of Scripture, and by what means can we learn to profit more?

These questions, which are so fundamental to Christian experience and happiness, provide the theme for this book by Arthur Pink. Originally published as a series in *Studies in the Scriptures*, a monthly magazine edited by the author for over 30 years, it has all the characteristics which have, since the author's death in 1952, led to his recognition as one of the finest Christian writers of the twentieth century. Certainly the present book is among his best and will be a help to Christians both young and old.

ISBN 0 85151 032 9
128pp. Paperback

JONAH
A Study in Compassion
O. Palmer Robertson

The Old Testament story catches the imagination and tells of a prophet who disobeys God and of a great fish which can swallow a man; it describes a city-wide revolt in a pagan country and a wonderfully-sighted prophet sulking in the sunshine. What does it mean?

In *Jonah: A Study in Compassion*, Dr O. Palmer Robertson's masterly knowledge of the Hebrew language, his vivid sense of the grace of God and the twisted state of a man's heart, and his ability to retell historical events and see their significance all combine to explain what the message of the book of Jonah really is, and—since there is a string in the tail—what it really means for us today.

ISBN 0 85151 575 4
64pp. Paperback

THE THOUGHT OF GOD

Maurice Roberts

This is a collection of articles which have already been widely read and appreciated as editorials in *The Banner of Truth* magazine, of which Maurice Roberts is the editor. Pointedly biblical, they are thoughtful and searching, humbling and exalting, challenging and encouraging.

Like editorials in other journals, Maurice Roberts' articles have spoken to the needs of the times. But while many editorials appear to have only historical or sociological interest at a later date, in contrast these are of lasting value. They have God and his Word as their starting place; and their horizon stretches beyond time to eternity. Those who have already read them will rejoice to have these pieces conveniently and permanently in book form, while those who come to them for the first time will appreciate their freshness, relevance and power, and will find in them a seriousness which has a sanctifying effect on the heart and a clarifying influence on the spiritual vision.

ISBN 0 85151 658 0
256pp. Paperback

WHAT'S WRONG WITH PREACHING TODAY?

A.N. Martin

The Christian church today stands in need of a recovery of good preaching. But how is that to take place? Part of the remedy lies in seeking to answer the question, What has gone wrong with preaching? The ability to analyse the weaknesses of contemporary preaching (and preachers) is essential to developing healthy and fruitful preaching.

In answering this vital question, Dr A. N. Martin draws on his own experience as a pastor and preacher and on the widespread opportunities he has had to teach and counsel other preachers. Fundamentally, however, his response is rooted in the biblical teaching on the character of those who preach and the message they are to proclaim. *What's Wrong With Preaching Today?* contains a searching message which will disturb complacency; but rather than create despair, it challenges all who preach (as well as those who hear) to rise to new levels of faithfulness and usefulness in the service of Christ.

ISBN 0 85151 007 8
32pp. Booklet

For further details and a free illustrated catalogue please write to:
THE BANNER OF TRUTH TRUST
3 Murrayfield Road, Edinburgh EH12 6EL
P.O. Box 621, Carlisle, Pennsylvania, 17013, U.S.A.